Psychological
Disorders

Schizophrenia

Psychological
Disorders

DATE DUE

NOV 1 2 2009		
NOV 2 0 2009		
MAY 0 7 2013 DEC 0 9 2013		
JAN 0 6 2013		
MAY 2 2 2014		
MAR 0 4 2015		
DEC - 4 2019		

Psychological Disorders

Schizophrenia

Heather Barnett Veague, Ph.D.

Series Editor
Christine Collins, Ph.D.
Research Assistant Professor of Psychology
Vanderbilt University

Foreword by
Pat Levitt, Ph.D.
Director, Vanderbilt Kennedy Center
for Research on Human Development

CHELSEA HOUSE
PUBLISHERS
An imprint of Infobase Publishing

Psychological Disorders: Schizophrenia

Chelsea House
An imprint of Infobase Publishing
132 West 31st Street
New York NY 10001

Library of Congress Cataloging-in-Publication Data
Veague, Heather Barnett.
    Schizophrenia / Heather Barnett Veague ; foreword by Pat Levitt.
        p. cm. — (Psychological disorders)
    Includes bibliographical references.
    ISBN-13: 978-0-7910-8544-8
    ISBN-10: 0-7910-8544-9
    1. Schizophrenia—Juvenile literature. I. Title. II. Series.
    RC514.V43 2007
    616.89'8—dc22   2007010057

Chelsea House books are available at special discounts when purchased in
bulk quantities for businesses, associations, institutions, or sales promotions.
Please call our Special Sales Department in New York at (212) 967-8800 or
 (800) 322-8755.

You can find Chelsea House on the World Wide Web at http://www.chelseahouse.com

Text and cover design by Keith Trego

Printed in the United States of America

Bang EJB 10 9 8 7 6 5 4 3 2 1

This book is printed on acid-free paper.

All links and Web addresses were checked and verified to be correct at the time of
publication. Because of the dynamic nature of the Web, some addresses and links
may have changed since publication and may no longer be valid.

Table of Contents

Foreword

Pat Levitt, Ph.D.
Vanderbilt Kennedy
Center for Research
on Human Development

Think of the most complicated aspect of our universe, and then multiply that by infinity! Even the most enthusiastic of mathematicians and physicists acknowledge that the brain is by far the most challenging entity to understand. By design, the human brain is made up of billions of cells called neurons, which use chemical neurotransmitters to communicate with each other through connections called synapses. Each brain cell has about 2,000 synapses. Connections between neurons are not formed in a random fashion, but rather are organized into a type of architecture that is far more complex than any of today's supercomputers. And, not only is the brain's connective architecture more complex than any computer; its connections are capable of *changing* to improve the way a circuit functions. For example, the way we learn new information involves changes in circuits that actually improve performance. Yet some change can also result in a disruption of connections, like changes that occur in disorders such as drug addiction, depression, schizophrenia, and epilepsy, or even changes that can increase a person's risk of suicide.

Genes and the environment are powerful forces in building the brain during development and ensuring normal brain functioning, but they can also be the root causes of psychological and neurological disorders when things go awry. The way in which brain architecture is built before birth and in childhood will determine how well the brain functions when we are adults, and even how susceptible we are to such diseases as depression, anxiety, or attention disorders, which can severely disturb brain function. In a sense, then, understanding how the brain is built can lead us to a clearer picture of the ways in which our brain works, how we can improve its functioning, and what we can do to repair it when diseases strike.

Brain architecture reflects the highly specialized jobs that are performed by human beings, such as seeing, hearing, feeling, smelling, and moving. Different brain areas are specialized to control specific functions. Each specialized area must communicate well with other areas for the brain to accomplish even more complex tasks, like controlling body physiology—our patterns of sleep, for example, or even our eating habits, both of which can become disrupted if brain development or function is disturbed in some way. The brain controls our feelings, fears, and emotions; our ability to learn and store new information; and how well we recall old information. The brain does all this, and more, by building, during development, the circuits that control these functions, much like a hard-wired computer. Even small abnormalities that occur during early brain development through gene mutations, viral infection, or fetal exposure to alcohol can increase the risk of developing a wide range of psychological disorders later in life.

Those who study the relationship between brain architecture and function, and the diseases that affect this bond, are neuroscientists. Those who study and treat the disorders that are caused by changes in brain architecture and chemistry are psychiatrists and psychologists. Over the last 50 years, we have learned quite a lot about how brain architecture and chemistry work and how genetics contribute to brain structure and function. Genes are very important in controlling the initial phases of building the brain. In fact, almost every gene in the human genome is needed to build the brain. This process of brain development actually starts prior to birth, with almost all the neurons we will ever have in our brain produced by mid-gestation. The assembly of the architecture, in the form of intricate circuits, begins by this time, and by birth, we have the basic organization laid out. But the work is not yet complete, because billions of connections form over a remarkably long period of time, extending through puberty. The brain of a child is being built and modified on a daily basis, even during sleep.

While there are thousands of chemical building blocks, such as proteins, lipids, and carbohydrates, that are used, much like bricks and mortar, to put the architecture together, the highly detailed connectivity that emerges during childhood depends greatly upon experiences and our environment. In building a house, we use specific blueprints to assemble the basic structures, like a foundation, walls, floors, and ceilings. The brain is assembled similarly. Plumbing and electricity, like the basic circuitry of the brain, are put in place early in the building process. But for all of this early work, there is another very important phase of development, which is termed experience-dependent development. During the first three years of life, our brains actually form far more connections than we will ever need, almost 40 percent more! Why would this occur? Well, in fact, the early circuits form in this way so that we can use experience to mold our brain architecture to best suit the functions that we are likely to need for the rest of our lives

Experience is not just important for the circuits that control our senses. A young child who experiences toxic stress, like physical abuse, will have his or her brain architecture changed in regions that will result in poorer control of emotions and feelings as an adult. Experience is powerful. When we repeatedly practice on the piano or shoot a basketball hundreds of times daily, we are using experience to model our brain connections to function at their finest. Some will achieve better results than others, perhaps because the initial phases of circuit-building provided a better base, just like the architecture of houses may differ in terms of their functionality. We are working to understand the brain structure and function that result from the powerful combination of genes building the initial architecture and a child's experience adding the all-important detailed touches. We also know that, like an old home, the architecture can break down. The aging process can be particularly hard on the ability of brain circuits to function at their best because positive change comes less readily as we get older. Synapses may be lost and brain chemistry can change over time. The difficulties in understanding how architecture gets built are paralleled by the complexities of what happens to that architecture as we grow older. Dementia associated with brain deterioration as a complication of Alzheimer's disease and memory loss associated with aging or alcoholism are active avenues of research in the neuroscience community.

There is truth, both for development and in aging, in the old adage "use it or lose it." Neuroscientists are pursuing the idea that brain architecture and chemistry can be modified well beyond childhood. If we understand the mechanisms that make it easy for a young, healthy brain to learn or repair itself following an accident, perhaps we can use those same tools to optimize the functioning of aging brains. We already know many ways in which we can improve the functioning of the aging or injured brain. For example, for an individual who has suffered a stroke that has caused structural damage to brain architecture, physical exercise can be quite powerful in helping to reorganize circuits so that they function better, even in an elderly individual. And you know that when you exercise and sleep regularly, you just feel better. Your brain chemistry and architecture are functioning at their best. Another example of ways we can improve nervous system function are the drugs that are used to treat mental illnesses. These drugs are designed to change brain chemistry so that the neurotransmitters used for communication between brain cells can function more normally. These same types of drugs, however, when taken in excess or abused, can actually damage brain chemistry and change brain architecture so that it functions more poorly.

As you read the Psychological Disorders series, the images of altered brain organization and chemistry will come to mind in thinking about complex diseases such as schizophrenia or drug addiction. There is nothing more fascinating and important to understand for the well-being of humans. But also keep in mind that as neuroscientists, we are on a mission to comprehend human nature, the way we perceive the world, how we recognize color, why we smile when thinking about the Thanksgiving turkey, the emotion of experiencing our first kiss, or how we can remember the winner of the 1953 World Series. If you are interested in people, and the world in which we live, you are a neuroscientist, too.

Pat Levitt, Ph.D.
Director, Vanderbilt Kennedy Center
for Research on Human Development
Vanderbilt University
Nashville, Tennessee

Introduction

The word *schizophrenia* conjures images of a nightmare world where strange and twisted realities exist. Schizophrenia is a brain disorder that can be so devastating, and has such a dark history, that its very name can be frightening. But the past several decades have brought increasing hope to patients and their families. Research on schizophrenia is beginning to uncover its causes, and treatments now bring stability to some patients' lives. Though some people with schizophrenia struggle with the disease throughout their lives, many can manage their condition with treatment and support, and their lives can be relatively independent and productive.

WHAT IS SCHIZOPHRENIA?

Schizophrenia, a complex and often disabling mental illness, is among the most serious of brain diseases. Because the term *schizophrenia* literally means "split mind," it is often confused with a "split," or multiple, personality. Schizophrenia, however, is a **psychotic** disorder that causes severe mental disturbances that disrupt thoughts, speech, and behavior. Despite its devastating effect on people who suffer from it, schizophrenia is difficult to diagnose. There is a broad range of symptoms that a schizophrenic might display, but no unique characteristic symptom. In general, a person with schizophrenia has disordered thinking and may attract attention with his behavior.

For example, someone with schizophrenia might mumble to themselves or dress in a way that is inappropriate for the season, such as wearing a heavy coat in summer. Some schizophrenics show symptoms such as withdrawal, apathy, **hallucinations,** or **delusions.** Certain symptoms tend to occur in clusters within a patient. Psychiatrists consider schizophrenia to be a group of related illnesses or a complex illness with subtypes, each characterized by a particular cluster of symptoms. The subtypes include Paranoid, Disorganized, Catatonic, and Residual. (See Chapter 2 for further description.) In addition, some patients are diagnosed with "undifferentiated schizophrenia" because their symptoms do not fall into one of the more common clusters that characterize the other major subtypes. There are no biological tests, such as blood tests, that can diagnose schizophrenia. A patient must be thoroughly evaluated by a psychiatrist, and even then **misdiagnoses** are common. Several other illnesses, such as bipolar disorder and schizoaffective disorder, have some of the same symptoms as schizophrenia and are sometimes confused with it.

HISTORY OF SCHIZOPHRENIA

We know that people through the centuries have suffered from schizophrenia. Archaeologists have found writings describing schizophrenic-like behaviors and symptoms from as far back as ancient Egyptian civilization. The earliest account of a mental illness that clearly refers to schizophrenia was written in 1656. In the late nineteenth century, Emil Kraepelin, a German psychiatrist, first characterized schizophrenia, describing its symptoms and claiming that damage to the brain was its cause. He called it "dementia praecox," or premature dementia, because he believed that patients suffered a continuous, irreversible mental deterioration starting early in life. Kraepelin's contemporary Eugen Bleuler disagreed. He felt that patients could show

Figure 1.1 Emil Kraepelin, a German psychiatrist, provided the first characterization of schizophrenia, in the late nineteenth century. He believed that the disorder was caused by irreversible physical damage to the brain. *National Library of Medicine*

improvement with treatment. He called the disease "schizophrenia," derived from the Greek words *schizo*, or "split," and *phrenia*, or "mind," because he believed it was characterized by a split, or mismatch, between different "psychic functions" such as thought and emotion. He described "the four A's," features that he felt defined the illness: lack of **affect**, or emotion; irrational or disorganized **associations**; **ambivalence** in attitudes and feelings; and **autism**, or retreat into an internal world. Bleuler believed that schizophrenia was not caused by physical damage to the brain but by a psychosocial disturbance.

Kraepelin and Bleuler's studies of patients with schizophrenia were the first steps toward our current understanding of the disease, but their conclusions led to some misunderstandings more harmful than helpful. Followers of Kraepelin who believed that schizophrenia was progressive and irreversible felt that treatment was fruitless and advocated permanent institutionalization of patients. Followers of Bleuler's views, on the other hand, believed that the condition was caused by psychological trauma during the patient's childhood. Out of this view came the concept of the "schizophrenogenic mother," or a mother who caused schizophrenia in her child through her style of parenting. By the 1960s and '70s, research had shown that neither of these was really true. Contrary to Kraepelin's claims, schizophrenia does not lead to an inevitable decline but follows a course that includes one or multiple psychotic episodes with periods of relative stability in between. In fact, symptoms might lessen or even disappear as the patient grows older. Although stress and emotion in the life of a schizophrenic may worsen the severity of symptoms, they are not the underlying cause of the disease, as Bleuler's followers claimed.

Beginning in the 1970s and continuing through to the present, we have made important advances in our understanding of schizophrenia. Old notions of its causes have been discredited and old treatments have been discarded. One of the earliest "treatments" for schizophrenia in Western medicine was institutionalization. Starting in the late 1600s, the mentally ill

Figure 1.2 Eugen Bleuler, a contemporary of Emil Kraepelin, believed that schizophrenia was caused by psychological trauma sustained early in life. *National Library of Medicine.*

were kept in hospitals, not to cure them, but to remove them from society. Often, patients were little more than prisoners in the institutions, and were very poorly treated. In fact, many of the mentally ill were simply thrown in jails. Through the 1700s and 1800s, attitudes did change, along with conditions in the hospitals. The hospitalized mentally ill were cared for much more humanely, and counseling was offered as treatment.

In the 1900s, psychiatrists began to look for ways to alter the functioning of the brain to treat mental illness. Treatments were developed that were used in hospitals to calm schizophrenics and other patients and reduce the delusions and hallucinations that agitated them. Three commonly practiced methods were insulin shock or insulin coma therapy, electroconvulsive therapy, and **lobotomy**. Insulin coma therapy involved administering high enough levels of insulin to induce a coma. A shot of glucose would bring patients out of the coma, and, when they awoke, they were left slow and lethargic. In electroconvulsive therapy, the patient's brain is given repeated sessions of electrical shock in order to alter brain activity. The altered electrical activity in the brain can change the patient's emotional state. Lobotomy surgically disrupts connections between the frontal lobes—parts of the brain critical to thought and emotion. The surgery left patients calmer but could also alter memory, intelligence, and personality. Although these methods sound more like torture than treatment today, there were few alternatives at the time. Despite terrible side effects associated with the treatments—including possible death from insulin coma therapy—these were considered effective ways of helping patients. In fact, electroconvulsive therapy is still used today and has been found to be effective in treating the most severe forms of **major depression**.

In the 1950s, psychiatrists began to use drugs to treat schizophrenia. Initially, tranquilizers were used simply to calm and subdue patients. The first medication that actually treated the symptoms of schizophrenia was the antipsychotic drug **chlorpromazine**, or Thorazine. Thorazine was a revolutionary treatment because patients on the drug could leave the hospital. Thorazine does not cure patients, but it does allow them to lead

Figure 1.3 Female patient chained to a post in an 18th century mental asylum. Methods of constraint such as this were often used because patients were seen as dangerous and it made the job easier for the few wardens assigned to watch them. © *SPL/Photo Researchers, Inc.*

John Forbes Nash Jr.

Not all we know about schizophrenia is dark and fearful. Even in the past, when effective treatments were not yet available, many schizophrenics could live many years of their lives relatively free from the devastating symptoms. As Bleuler pointed out almost 100 years ago, the course of the disease is not a one-way downward slide. The story of one of the most famous people who has suffered from schizophrenia makes that clear and gives many people hope.

John Forbes Nash Jr. is a brilliant mathematician who won a Nobel Prize in Economics. You might recognize his name from the popularity of a movie loosely based on his biography, *A Beautiful Mind*, by Sylvia Nasar. Nash completed his education, started a career as a professor, and married before he developed schizophrenia. In 1958, at the age of 30, Nash developed paranoid delusions that the government was plotting against him. Against his will, he was committed to McLean hospital in Massachusetts. While in the hospital, Nash was given antipsychotic medication. After leaving the hospital, he soon quit taking the medication because of the side effects, and the paranoid delusions returned. Over the next 12 years, Nash was in and out of mental hospitals where he was treated with drugs and insulin coma therapy. He showed temporary improvement after each hospitalization but always deteriorated again to a delusional state. During this time, he lost his job, his marriage, and his home.

In 1974, Nash's wife took him into her home, near Princeton University. Because of his reputation and the friendships he had made before his illness, Nash was allowed to spend his days wandering around the university, where people left him alone or ignored his odd behaviors. He lived in his own world within Princeton, refusing medication but avoiding hospitalization, for almost two decades.

Figure 1.4 John Nash pictured at Princeton University. After his schizophrenia went into remission, he was able to accept his Nobel Prize and return to work. © *Najilah Feanny/Corbis SABA*

Then, in the 1990s, Nash began to escape from his hallucinations and delusional thinking and his schizophrenia went into remission. By 1994, he was well enough to travel to Sweden to accept the Nobel Prize that was awarded for his early work. In 2001, he remarried his ex-wife and began to make contact with long-lost family. He took up his work again and restarted his brilliant career, making new and important contributions to the field of mathematics.

What accounts for John Nash's stunning recovery? Nash himself believes that he reasoned himself out of his illness, that he overcame his hallucinations and delusions through

(continues)

(continued)

intellect. In an interview for a public television program, he said: "I began arguing with the concept of the voices. And ultimately I began rejecting them and deciding not to listen."[1] In his autobiography for the Nobel Prize, he wrote: "[G]radually I began to intellectually reject some of the delusionally influenced lines of thinking which had been characteristic of my orientation."[2] His biographer, Nasar, believes that it was the support of his family and friends and the tolerance and protection of the Princeton community that allowed Nash to recover. She wrote of his time wandering the halls of Princeton, "To have his delusions seen not just as bizarre and unintelligible, but as having intrinsic value, was surely one aspect of these 'lost years' that paved the way for an eventual remission."[3] And interviewed for the same public television program, she said, "The fact that people did not abandon him, that there were people who treated him like a human being, made it possible for him to re-emerge."[4]

Although it is certainly true that family and community support can help people with schizophrenia deal better with the illness, support networks cannot cure the disease. Remission from schizophrenia is not something that only Nash's unusual circumstances at Princeton—or his extraordinary intellect—could bring about. E. Fuller Torrey, a psychiatrist and renowned expert on schizophrenia has said, "We know as a general rule, with exceptions, that as people with schizophrenia age, they have fewer symptoms, such as delusions and hallucinations. . . . So that when Nash hits his late forties and fifties, and his life gets better, it's not shocking at all. Anyone who follows the literature would never characterize it as a miracle."[5] Nash's recovery was not yet another astonishing accomplishment of a remarkable man, but the normal course of his disease, and an outcome for which all sufferers of schizophrenia may hope.

a more normal life that is not controlled by psychotic symptoms. Although it has serious side effects, it was safer and far more helpful than any treatment that had been used before it. Since the introduction of Thorazine, even more effective drugs have been developed (Chapter 5), but still no cure. The best medications improve many symptoms but also have unpleasant side effects. The goal of modern pharmaceutical science is to design drugs that target atypical brain functions and leave all others unaffected. Finding the best treatments for schizophrenia will require a better understanding of its causes.

WHO SUFFERS FROM SCHIZOPHRENIA?

According to the National Institute for Mental Health, Schizophrenia strikes one percent of the population worldwide, including approximately 2.2 million people in the United States. It is not the most common mental illness: The National Alliance on Mental Illness reports that bipolar disorder affects 1.2 percent of adult Americans; **obsessive compulsive disorder** affects 2 percent; and major depression affects 5 percent each year.[6] Nonetheless, most of the people in psychiatric hospitals are in treatment for schizophrenia.

New and promising theories suggest potential causes of schizophrenia (Chapter 4) and ideas on how to treat it. Researchers have asked such questions as, "Why do some people develop schizophrenia while others do not? What do people who develop schizophrenia have in common?" We know that schizophrenia occurs worldwide, and at approximately the same frequency, one percent of the population, everywhere it has been studied. There are no differences in the prevalence of schizophrenia by race, ethnicity, culture, or religion. This suggests that these factors play little role in the development of the disease. Schizophrenia occurs at the same rate in males and females, though there are some sex differences in the expression of the disease. On average, males seem to be more severely disabled than females.

Are there any groups of people who are more likely than others to develop schizophrenia? In fact, the people most likely to develop schizophrenia are the relatives of schizophrenics. This suggests that schizophrenia has a **genetic** cause. But genes are not the whole answer. We know that for two people with exactly the same genes—identical twins—if one is schizophrenic, the other has less than a 50 percent chance of also developing schizophrenia. Also, people who appear to have no schizophrenic relatives at all may still develop the disease. This tells us that the environment also plays a role in the development of schizophrenia.

In this book you will read about how to identify someone with schizophrenia, what symptoms make up the disease, and how clinicians diagnose patients. You will learn about the many factors that influence the development of schizophrenia. So far, we do not know the *cause* of schizophrenia, but we do know many things that increase a person's likelihood of developing it. You will also read about various treatments for schizophrenia. A combination of medication, therapy, and community support has been shown to be the most effective treatment for the disease. Finally, you will read about how schizophrenia affects families and society.

Diagnosing Schizophrenia

Emilio is a 40-year-old man who came to the hospital with his mother. He is dressed in a dirty coat, bedroom slippers, and a baseball cap and has several medals hanging around his neck. He appears to be angry at his mother, claiming that she is poisoning him. Sometimes he giggles and acts seductively toward the interviewer. He talks like a child and walks with a swing in his step and exaggerated hip movements. His mother tells the interviewer that Emilio stopped taking his medication a month ago and that since then, he has begun to hear voices and act more and more bizarrely. When he is asked what he has been doing lately, he responds, "eating wires and lighting fires." His speech is difficult to understand and he often rhymes his words even if the rhymes do not make sense.

Emilio dropped out of high school when he was 16. He was hospitalized because he was hearing voices telling him that the principal of his high school was trying to kill him. Emilio receives medications for his symptoms during every hospitalization. Within a few months, however, he often stops taking his medications and eventually returns to the hospital. He lives with his mother but occasionally leaves her house and disappears for months at a time. On these occasions, Emilio has been picked up by the police for his behavior and returned to a psychiatric hospital.[7]

Emilio's behaviors worry his mother. Like many patients with schizophrenia, Emilio was first brought to the hospital at an early age. Although many patients receive psychiatric treatment early, it often takes many visits over many years for a psychiatrist to determine the proper diagnosis of schizophrenia and decide on an appropriate treatment regimen. In fact, according to one study, there is an average delay of 10 years from the first onset of symptoms to correct diagnosis and treatment of psychiatric disorders. For schizophrenia specifically, the time lag between the appearance of the first sign of a mental disorder and the first hospital admission with the diagnosis of schizophrenia averages over six years.[8] In order for a patient with schizophrenia to receive proper treatment, mental health professionals must be able to identify a pattern of behaviors, or symptoms, of the disease. Once the symptoms are identified, a diagnosis is made and treatment can begin.

SYMPTOM CATEGORIES

Schizophrenia is a disease that does not discriminate based on race, culture, social status, or gender. Anywhere in the world, in every culture, one person out of every hundred suffers from schizophrenia. Signs of schizophrenia may emerge in people as young as 15 or as late as one's forties, but it is most common for true psychotic symptoms to reveal themselves in the late teens and early twenties. Indeed, Emilio appears to follow this pattern. His bizarre behaviors began in high school, with his first psychiatric hospitalization soon following. Interestingly, men seem to develop schizophrenia at an earlier age than women. The average age of onset of schizophrenia in men is 25 years, whereas 29 is the average age for women. Certain traits, such as having a relative with schizophrenia, increase a person's risk of developing the disease. We will discuss risk factors for schizophrenia in Chapter 4.

There are three categories of schizophrenic symptoms: positive, negative, and disorganized. Dr. E. Fuller Torrey, in his book

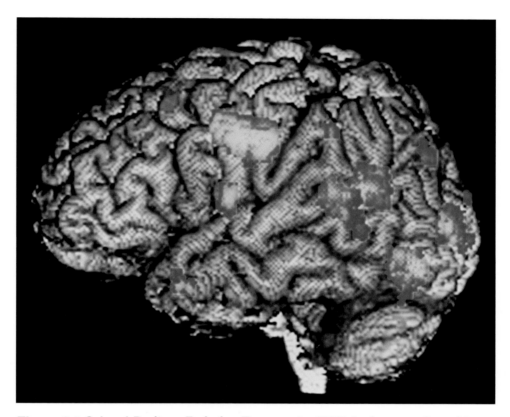

Figure 2.1 Colored Positron Emission Tomography (PET) brain scan of a schizo-phrenic male patient during hallucination. Highlighted in orange are the active visual (at right) and auditory (upper center) areas of the brain, confirming that the patient has "seen and heard" a hallucination. © *D. Silbersweig/Photo Researchers, Inc.*

Surviving Schizophrenia, explained that the adjective *positive* ". . . denotes those symptoms which are present and should be absent." In simple terms, a **positive symptom** signals a behavior that shouldn't be there. Remember that *positive* as used here does not mean "good." An example of a positive symptom is hallucination. Hallucinations occur when someone hears, sees, smells, or feels things that are not really there. Emilio is hearing voices and although we do not know what they are saying, they seem to be contributing to his erratic behavior.

Another positive symptom is delusion. Delusions cause the patient to believe that people are reading their thoughts or plotting against them, that others are secretly monitoring and threatening them, or that they can control other people's minds. Emilio believes that his mother is poisoning him, even though this is not true. This is an example of a paranoid delusion.

Negative symptoms reflect the absence of certain normal characteristics and behaviors.[9] An example of this is **blunted affect**, which means that someone does not show an appropriate range of emotions. For example, someone with blunted affect might not laugh at a joke that most people would find funny.

Other examples of negative symptoms include an inability to start and follow through with activities, speech that is brief and lacks content, and a lack of pleasure or interest in life. Someone with schizophrenia may have such little energy that he or she can do nothing other than sleep or eat. Blunted affect means that many individuals with schizophrenia may seem like they don't have feelings. Remember that just because a patient doesn't show emotion does not mean that he or she doesn't feel it. People working with schizophrenia patients must continue to be sensitive to their feelings and treat them with kindness and consideration. Social withdrawal may also be a symptom of schizophrenia. Many patients fear being with other people or believe that they simply cannot keep up with other people so they prefer to be alone. This isolation may contribute to depression in schizophrenia and prevent patients from seeking treatment.

Some patients with negative symptoms also exhibit certain physical behaviors. They might move extremely slowly, make repetitive gestures or walk in circles or pace. Emilio demonstrates some disorganized movements when he walks with exaggerated hip movements and a swing in his step.

Disorganized symptoms include odd and confused thinking, speech, and behavior. Emilio exhibits several disorganized symptoms. To begin, he is dressed in a dirty coat, baseball cap, and bedroom slippers. His speech is slurred and he talks like a child and often uses rhyme, as exhibited by his description of his recent activities as "eating wires and lighting fires." Rhymes that don't make sense are called **clang associations**.

Schizophrenia is also associated with changes in cognition. Cognition is the way we perceive and think about things. People with schizophrenia may have problems remembering things and find it difficult to plan for the future. Many patients with schizophrenia have problems focusing their attention on a task for more than a brief period of time. Motivation is absent in many of these patients and they often feel that many goals are simply out of their reach. Research has indicated that the cognitive problems of schizophrenia may be important factors in determining treatment **outcome.** Outcome is a general measure of how well a patient is functioning over the long-term.

Many individuals affected with schizophrenia become depressed or have clinically significant mood swings. People with schizophrenia may experience symptoms of depression such as feeling hopeless or believing that life has no meaning. Some patients have feelings of guilt for the trouble they have caused for their family members and friends and they may feel unworthy and unlovable. In extreme cases, a person with schizophrenia may become so depressed that they wish to end their life. They may talk of suicide or even attempt to harm themselves. When mood instability is a major feature of schizophrenia, it is called **schizoaffective disorder.** In schizoaffective disorder, elements of schizophrenia and mood disorders are observed in the same individual. It is not clear whether schizoaffective disorder is a distinct condition or simply a subtype of schizophrenia. A mental health professional who is formulating a treatment plan for a patient with schizophrenia must consider mood as well as psychotic symptoms. In the next section, you will learn about specific symptoms within these symptom categories.

DIAGNOSTIC CRITERIA

All the behaviors you just read about may be symptoms of schizophrenia, although very few patients with schizophrenia exhibit all these symptoms. Instead, most individuals with the disease display a few of these symptoms. The set of symptoms a patient with schizophrenia experiences is called a **symptom profile**. In order to diagnose someone with schizophrenia, a clinician must determine that the person has exhibited at least *two* psychotic symptoms for at least six months. This does not mean that the psychotic symptoms must be continually present for six months, but rather that the symptoms have been present more often than not. A brief discussion of each of the five psychotic symptoms follows:

Delusions. A delusion is a false belief that cannot be explained by one's culture or social environment. Someone with a delusion cannot be dissuaded from this belief, despite evidence that it is not consistent with societal norms. There are several types of delusions. A **delusion of grandeur** is one in which the person believes that he or she is someone famous or very important such as God or a movie star. Alternatively, patients with this kind of delusion might believe that they are especially close to a celebrity or religious figure. Some patients have **delusions of guilt** in which they believe that they have committed a terrible crime or sin. Someone with schizophrenia might have a **somatic delusion** in which he or she believes that something terrible has happened to his or her body. For example, some people with schizophrenia believe they have developed cancer or that their intestines have been replaced with a garden hose. Perhaps the most common kind of delusion is a **persecutory delusion**.

A person with a persecutory delusion believes that someone or something is trying to hurt him or her. A **delusion of reference** causes patients to believe that they are being talked about, sometimes on the television or radio, or in the newspaper. Finally, some patients with schizophrenia experience delusions of **thought control**, in which they believe that thoughts are being put into or taken out of their minds.

Hallucinations. Hallucinations occur when someone perceives something that others cannot perceive. The most common form of hallucination is auditory, which involves hearing things others can't hear. Additionally, hallucinations may be visual, in which people believe they see something that no one else can see. **Tactile hallucinations** occur when an individual feels something that he or she can't explain, like the tingling of electricity for no reason. Rarely, schizophrenia patients experience **olfactory hallucinations** and smell things that other people cannot smell. Finally, few patients experience **gustatory hallucinations** and taste things that other people can't taste. The content of gustatory and olfactory hallucinations is usually unpleasant, like the smell or taste of garbage or something rotting.

Disorganized Speech. Perhaps the most puzzling symptom of schizophrenia is **disorganized speech**. Someone whose speech is disorganized is frequently off-topic and nearly impossible to understand. A patient might start talking about his or her mother and quickly change the subject and begin talking about apple orchards. The connection between the mother and apple orchards is usually only understood by the patient. That is, the patient may have started thinking of his mother, which led him to think about his childhood home, which was in New York City, which reminded him of the Empire State Building, which reminded him of Empire apples. A patient who is severely disorganized is even more difficult to understand. Someone who speaks in this way may construct a sentence like this, "There is nail polish on the pizza which sits on a truck, good luck!" Not only is this sentence nonsensical, but the last few words rhyme. As in the case study of Emilio, one form of disorganized speech is clang associations, or using rhyme inappropriately. The most extreme form of disorganized speech is called **word salad**. This is speech that is so disorganized that it makes no sense at all, literally or grammatically. An example of word salad is, "Run simple cake gate spilling baby." Interestingly, grossly disorganized speech is so contrary to regular language patterns that it is extremely difficult to mimic. Forming associations between words and objects is a natural behavior. It is so natural that it is nearly impossible to think of words that are completely unrelated.

Disorganized Behavior. In addition to speech, behavior may be disorganized and symptomatic of schizophrenia. Disorganized behavior means that the patient has difficulty with goal-oriented behavior. Patients who have disorganized behavior have problems dressing themselves or preparing food to eat. They often dress inappropriately, in clothes that are dirty or obviously mismatched. Some people with schizophrenia will go out in the winter in shorts and a T-shirt, or they will dress in a sweatshirt and overcoat in the summer. Other forms of disorganized behavior include shouting or cursing in public.

Negative Symptoms. The final category of psychotic symptoms is negative symptoms. Recall that negative symptoms refer to normal behaviors that some patients with schizophrenia lack. You may remember primary negative symptoms by thinking of the three As. The three As refer to anhedonia, avolition, and alogia. **Anhedonia** is an inability to enjoy activities, or in general to get pleasure out of life. These patients may have low energy and, as a result, spend a lot of time just sitting

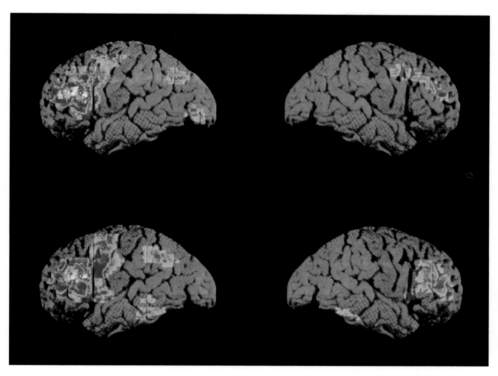

Figure 2.2 This PET scan of a schizophrenic verbal task shows activity in the brain of a schizophrenic (bottom) versus a healthy brain (top). The normal brain shows activity in the prefrontal and motor areas and less in the parietal area on the left side, whereas in the schizophrenic brain these areas are active with the added area of the temporal gyrus (lower center of brain). © *Wellcome/Photo Reasearchers, Inc.*

around or sleeping. Often, patients with negative symptoms are not interested in life in general and have little motivation to try new things. Having little motivation or persistence in beginning or completing tasks is called **avolition**. Another negative symptom is **alogia**, or a difficulty or inability to speak. Patients with alogia are very difficult to treat with therapy because they might never answer a question about how they are feeling or at least take a long time to do so. Patients with negative symptoms are rarely interested in or comfortable around other people. They lack social skills and experience difficulty interacting with others. Many patients with predominantly negative symptoms keep to themselves and withdraw from social activities.

In order to be diagnosed with schizophrenia, a patient must exhibit symptoms in at least two of the categories listed above. A patient may be diagnosed with schizophrenia, however, if he or she exhibits one of the following three behaviors, even in the absence of other symptoms:

1. If the patient's delusions are significantly bizarre, such as believing that the FBI is wiretapping one's

What Is It Like to Have Schizophrenia?

One negative symptom of schizophrenia is flat or blunted affect. Individuals with this symptom rarely show their emotions, even in the presence of apparently disturbing stimuli. Ann Kring and John Neale, professors at the State University of New York at Stony Brook, wanted to know if patients who didn't show their emotions also didn't feel emotions to the same extent as people without schizophrenia. These researchers took a group of schizophrenia patients and a group of healthy adults and showed each group three types of film clips. The film clips were intended to elicit very positive, very negative, or neutral emotions. While the participants were watching the film clips, the researchers videotaped them. Additionally, researchers measured the participants' autonomic arousal, or physical indicators of emotion (heartbeat is an example of a way in which we can measure autonomic arousal). Next, the participants were asked about what emotions they experienced apartment and that aliens are performing experiments on the patient at night.

2. When a patient experiences auditory hallucinations in which there are two voices talking to each other.

3. When a patient hears a voice keeping a running commentary on what the patient is doing. This means that the patient hears a voice saying things like, "Now you are going to the store to buy groceries. The woman at the checkout counter is looking at you because she knows you are bad." Patients who hear a running commentary generally can get little quiet from the voices in their head.

during the film. After the film clips were over and the participants went home, experienced raters watched the videotapes and noted the facial expressiveness of all the participants. Not surprisingly, the schizophrenia patients showed less facial expressiveness than the controls. That is, relative to the non-schizophrenic participants, they appeared to be indifferent to the film clips. The schizophrenia patients did indicate, however, that they were experiencing emotion on the other measures. When asked how they felt watching the film clips, participants with schizophrenia reported just as much if not more intense emotion than did the healthy participants. The physiological indicators were consistent with patients' self-report as their physiological reactivity exceeded that of the normal participants. This study provides promising evidence that, although schizophrenia patients may appear to be cold and indifferent, in fact they appear to have emotional experience quite similar to people without schizophrenia.

SUBTYPES OF SCHIZOPHRENIA

Once a patient is diagnosed with schizophrenia, a clinician considers his or her symptoms and determines a **subtype diagnosis**. There are four subtypes of schizophrenia. Each subtype is based upon the types of symptoms the patient experiences.

Paranoid Type. Although psychotic by definition, patients with paranoid type usually appear the most "normal." That is, they are generally able to take care of themselves and their behavior and physical appearance often remains unaffected. Patients with this type of schizophrenia may have intimate relationships with other people; it is not uncommon for them to marry and have children. Their primary symptoms include delusions and/or hallucinations. These patients do not experience any negative symptoms, meaning that they rarely lose the ability to talk clearly. Paranoid type generally develops later than other forms of schizophrenia and usually responds quite well to medication.

Disorganized Type. Patients with disorganized type are the most apparently psychotic. They are difficult to understand and their appearance makes them easy to identify. Someone with disorganized type schizophrenia might dress in weather-inappropriate clothing or appear disheveled and unkempt. The disorganized type of schizophrenia was first recognized more than 100 years ago by a German psychiatrist, Ewald Hecker. In 1871, Hecker identified a group of patients who demonstrated extremely psychotic behaviors beginning in late adolescence or early adulthood. He called this pattern **hebephrenia**, originating from the Greek word *hebe,* meaning "youth." Emilio, from the case study at the beginning of the chapter, appears to have schizophrenia, disorganized type.

Catatonic Type. Patients with **catatonic schizophrenia** may have symptoms similar to patients with other subtypes of the disease but their physical movements make them different. Catatonic behavior is typically extremely slow, and these patients may appear as though they are moving in slow motion. Sometimes these patients refuse to speak or even to acknowledge the presence of others. Such behaviors are called **negativistic**. Patients who have this form of schizophrenia may arrange their body in strange postures for extended periods of time. They may lie curled up in a ball for hours, their muscles so tense that it is nearly impossible for other people to move them. They may involuntarily mimic the speech of others, a behavior called **echolalia**. Alternatively, these patients may involuntarily mimic the behaviors of others, a behavior called **echopraxia**. In very rare cases, a patient with schizophrenia, catatonic type, may display random hyperactivity, purposeless exhibitions of manic-like behavior.

Undifferentiated Type. Schizophrenia, undifferentiated type is a category used for patients who do not meet the criteria for any other subtype. That is, these patients may meet the general minimum criteria for schizophrenia but do not exhibit a pattern of symptoms that is consistent with any subtype.

Schizophrenia patients may have symptoms that are part of more than one subtype. For example, Emilio appears to have both paranoid and disorganized symptoms, in that he believes his mother is trying to poison him, he is dressed strangely, and he uses odd words and rhymes to express himself. One type of symptom, however, often trumps another. For example, if a patient has any disorganized symptoms, even if he has a paranoid symptom, he will receive a diagnosis of schizophrenia, disorganized type. Similarly, if a patient has any symptoms of catatonia, even if he has disorganized or paranoid symptoms, he will receive a diagnosis of schizophrenia, catatonic type.

First-Person Schizophrenia

A leading academic journal in the area of schizophrenia research frequently publishes first-person accounts of people suffering from schizophrenia. The following text is adapted from one of these accounts, by Valerie Fox:

"Having suffered from schizophrenia for the past 30 years—including a period of homelessness—I know the complexity of the illness. When I was a young woman in my twenties, working for an airline and traveling throughout the world, my life was wonderful, exciting. I was part of the theater scene in New York, liked the fabulous restaurants there, and was thoroughly enjoying my life.

"One day, however, my life changed drastically. I was diagnosed with schizophrenia, hospitalized, and given medicine. When I was healthy enough to leave the hospital, I was overwhelmed. I could not believe the medicine was good for me, because I had never felt so depressed and lethargic as I did while taking the medicine. After a few months I decided to stop taking the medicine, believing, as my psychiatrist did, that I would be fine, that I had been struggling with the transition from teenager to young womanhood, and that my "breakdown" would probably never recur. This was the thinking in the 1960s. There was no talk then of body chemistry being involved with schizophrenia.

"I did go off my medicine about six months after my first episode. I felt great: I had my alertness, my good sense of who I was; I was not depressed; and I looked forward to working again. Instead, within weeks I was again hospitalized. This time I was sent to a long-term care facility, a state hospital. During this time I decided to take charge of my life. I realized that when I was taking the medicine I was able to stay in the community; without the medicine, I was institutionalized. I determined I would find a way to cope with taking the medicine, because I did not want my life to be a revolving door from society to the hospital and back again.

"While in remission I met a good man and discussed with my doctor the feasibility of my getting married and having children. I did marry and gave birth to two children. During the course of the marriage, if we had an argument and I got angry, my husband would say, "Valerie, are you getting ill?" I wasn't getting ill, but my illness was a controlling factor for my husband to use over me. As this kept happening, I knew the marriage was over for me and that I would leave it as soon as my daughters were a little older. I did leave and retained custody of my two daughters. For 14 years, I remained healthy and was not re-hospitalized. I took my medicine and went to psychotherapy. I had gained a relative peace, acceptance, and a good level of happiness.

"Then came a dramatic schizophrenic episode. It started when someone began harassing me in the middle of the night. This harassment culminated with the person cutting my bedroom screen. I was terrified that because I slept so soundly as a result of the medicine, I would awaken one night with a stranger in my apartment. I decided to stop taking my medicine against the advice of my doctor. I had to do what I thought was responsible, and that was to be semi-awake in case an intruder entered my apartment. The police finally staked out my apartment and apprehended the person who was harassing me, but the damage was done. Because I was an adult and not acting out, I was free from forced hospitalization. I did not know I was ill. My ex-husband took our children, which I thought was

(continues)

(continued)

kidnapping. No one would help me have the children returned. I must have been visibly ill, although I was not aware of it.

"I went deeper and deeper into schizophrenia, ending in homelessness for a two-year period. During this period of homelessness and mental illness, I faced the dangers of street living, including being beaten and raped, almost freezing to death, and being malnourished, but I was free. In that state, freedom was what I wanted. This odyssey ended one day when I decided to do whatever it took to have the good life I had known. I still did not know I was ill, but I did associate taking medicine and being hospitalized with living as I had previously, before homelessness.

"One day, I summoned every bit of strength I had and did not back away from institutionalization. Fortunately, the psychiatrist I saw during the admittance process treated me with empathy, compassion, and respect. I trusted him, and, therefore, did not back away from my decision to seek treatment. I remained hospitalized for a six-month period, three months of which were spent waiting for a bed in a housing program in the community. Eventually, I reunited with my children and built another life for myself. I still see a therapist and can call between visits if I am very upset. I don't abuse this arrangement, and it has served me very well."

MISDIAGNOSIS, OR OTHER DISORDERS THAT MAY LOOK LIKE SCHIZOPHRENIA

It is crucial to realize that schizophrenia is not the cause of all psychotic symptoms. *Psychosis* is a general term used to describe psychotic symptoms whereas schizophrenia is a type of psychosis. In addition to schizophrenia, psychotic symptoms may result from a variety of causes, including brain trauma, strokes, tumors, infections, or the use of illegal drugs. Misdiagnosis is common in schizophrenia for precisely this reason. Mental health professionals may require several months (or years) in order to determine that the cause of psychotic symptoms is schizophrenia and not some other condition.

Indeed, assessing a patient with psychotic symptoms can be a challenging task. Clinicians and researchers typically go through a process of "ruling out" other disorders before confirming a diagnosis. In addition to brain trauma, there are other mental disorders in which symptoms appear very similar to those of schizophrenia. Sometimes there are more appropriate diagnoses for individuals with psychotic symptoms. For example, some patients with psychotic symptoms also have depression. When this is the case, a clinician must consider a diagnosis of schizoaffective disorder. Alternatively, the use of some illegal drugs may mimic psychotic symptoms. In order to determine that the symptoms are truly those of schizophrenia, it is important to determine that the patient has not been using substances that can cause these behaviors. Some other disorders in which psychotic symptoms are prominent follow.

Schizoaffective Disorder. Schizoaffective disorder is characterized by both schizophrenia and severe mood disorder symptoms. Someone with schizoaffective disorder meets diagnostic criteria for schizophrenia and at the same time experiences severe moods and marked changes of mood.

Schizophreniform Disorder. In order to receive a diagnosis of schizophrenia, one must exhibit psychotic symptoms for at least six months. Alternatively, a diagnosis of schizophreniform disorder is used when patients have only experienced these symptoms between one and six months. Presumably, every schizophrenia patient was a candidate for a diagnosis of schizophreniform disorder, as it is basically the same thing as schizophrenia, only for a shorter period of time.

Delusional Disorder. People with delusional disorder endorse beliefs that are have no grounding in reality. Contrary to schizophrenia, however, delusional disorder is not marked by extreme behavior change or disorganized behavior. Patients with delusional disorder can function normally, except for their behaviors brought about by their delusions. An example of a common form of delusion seen in delusional disorder is erotomania. Patients with erotomania believe that they are involved in a love affair with someone, even if this is not true. It is not uncommon for people with erotomania to believe they are having a relationship with a movie star or a famous politician.

Brief Psychotic Disorder. Brief psychotic disorder involves the sudden development of psychotic symptoms and rarely lasts for more than a few days. Typically, these episodes are brought about by an extremely stressful event, such as the death or infidelity of a spouse or the loss of a job. After the psychotic symptoms remit, they rarely return and the person returns to normal. Brief psychotic disorder is very rare and not often seen in clinical settings.

Shared Psychotic Disorder. Called *folie à deux* in French, shared psychotic disorder is perhaps the most puzzling of all these categories. Translated, *folie à deux* means "madness shared by two" and occurs when one person (let's call this person A) has a close relationship with someone who has a delusion (person B). Over time, person A begins to believe in person B's delusion and ultimately the two share the same delusion.

Drug-Induced Psychosis. Because the effects of some illegal drugs mimic psychotic symptoms, it is necessary to determine that a patient who is experiencing symptoms is not using drugs. Some drugs that can cause schizophrenia-like symptoms include cocaine, methamphetamine, and hallucinogens.

The Course of Schizophrenia

Kevin recently attended his first appointment at the mental health clinic. At 25 years of age, Kevin lives with his cousin Natalie and works for a radio station. Natalie is worried about Kevin because he is spending increasing amounts of time at home, locked in his room, playing loud music. When she asks him to turn it down Kevin just ignores her and buries his head under his pillow. Natalie encouraged Kevin to talk to someone about his problems and told him that he would have to move out of her house if he didn't get help soon. Kevin agreed to go see a therapist because he had nowhere else to live.

During the appointment, Kevin revealed some startling things. While working at the radio station, he became convinced that he heard his coworkers talking about him. He believed that his coworkers were calling him a liar and a thief. Kevin determined that they must have found out that he occasionally stole money out of his mother's purse when he was a young boy. Kevin believed that his coworkers were broadcasting a nighttime radio show that was all about him and all the bad things he had done. Further, Kevin believed that the show was raising thousands of advertising dollars that were being sent to the Middle East to fund terrorist groups. He felt terrible about this, and was convinced that there would be a terrorist attack soon because of the money the show about him raised.

Although Kevin never actually heard the show on the radio, he was convinced it was being broadcast. He believed that the disc jockeys were watching him and knew to air the show when Kevin couldn't listen to the radio. Lately, Kevin believed that he could hear the show when the radio wasn't on. In order to get away from the voices, Kevin blasted his music and sometimes hid his head under the pillow. Unfortunately, the voices were getting louder and louder and Kevin just couldn't escape them.

Kevin is an excellent example of a patient with schizophrenia, paranoid type. He experiences auditory hallucinations and delusions of reference and guilt. Recall that the average age for the first episode of schizophrenia in males is 25, exactly the age Kevin is now. In order to determine how best to treat Kevin's illness, a therapist would like to know about any early behaviors that might have predicted this episode and follow him closely for an extended period of time.

STAGES OF SCHIZOPHRENIA

Researchers have identified three stages of schizophrenia:

Prodromal Stage. The first stage is called the **prodromal stage** and refers to the year before the illness appears. The term prodrome is derived from the Greek word *prodromos*, meaning "something that comes before and signals an event".[10] In medical terms, a prodrome refers to the early symptoms and signs of an illness that come before the characteristic symptoms appear. For example, chicken pox is described as having a prodrome of a few days characterized by fever, headache, and loss of appetite. This is followed by the rash more commonly associated with chicken pox, making definitive diagnosis possible. People in the prodromal stage of schizophrenia often isolate themselves, stay alone in their bedroom a lot and stop spending time with family or friends. Their school or work performance suffers and they may show signs of decreased motivation, loss of interest in activities, and inappropriate or blunted emotions. The signs of the prodromal stage are not specific to schizophrenia. That is, someone who is experiencing these behaviors might be depressed or have some other problem. That is why one cannot identify the prodromal stage until the active phase is reached. Until a patient experiences psychotic symptoms, a physician cannot diagnose schizophrenia.

Interestingly, signs of the prodromal stage have been identified as early as childhood. Some innovative research by Elaine Walker and her colleagues at Emory University has involved examining childhood home movies of adults with schizophrenia, and without schizophrenia. Raters, who were unaware of which children had schizophrenia as adults, found that the children who were to develop schizophrenia as adults were often clumsy and awkward. Although clumsiness is not unique to children who will develop schizophrenia, this sign is seen significantly more often in children at risk for the disorder. Thus, signs of schizophrenia might be present several years before psychotic symptoms emerge.

Family members can be invaluable when it comes to identifying the prodrome of schizophrenia.[11] Relatives might sense that something "isn't quite right" with their family member, even if they're not certain whether it is just a bad mood, a normal developmental stage, or the influence of alcohol or illegal drugs.

Family members of patients with schizophrenia have identified several behaviors that indicated to them that something was wrong with their relative. Although the prodromal signs differ from patient to patient, nearly all family members of schizophrenia patients indicate that their relative experienced social withdrawal. Following, you will find 10 examples of behaviors that relatives of schizophrenia patients noticed in their family member during the prodromal stage of schizophrenia. Remember that many behaviors that are part of the prodrome are within the normal range of experience.

10 WARNING SIGNS OF SCHIZOPHRENIA AS IDENTIFIED BY FAMILY MEMBERS

1. Deterioration of personal hygiene
2. Sleeping excessively or inability to sleep
3. Unexpected hostility
4. Extreme preoccupation with religion or with the occult
5. Dropping out of activities—or out of life in general
6. Inappropriate laughter
7. Shaving head or body hair
8. Staring without blinking—or blinking incessantly
9. Peculiar use of words
10. Sensitivity and irritability when touched by others

Acute Stage. When someone is experiencing psychotic symptoms such as hallucinations, delusions, or grossly disorganized behavior, they are said to be in the acute or **active stage** of schizophrenia. The active phase indicates full development of the disorder. When patients are in the active phase, they appear psychotic. Their behavior may become so extreme or bizarre that hospitalization is necessary. Once a patient is brought to medical attention, a mental health professional will observe the patient, question the patient, and question the patient's family members if they are available. The goals of the first assessment are to ascertain when the strange behaviors began, how long they have lasted, and rule out the use of alcohol or drugs. Patients who are grossly psychotic are difficult to interview, so they might be treated with antipsychotic medication upon admission. Indeed, patients in the active phase of schizophrenia often need antipsychotic medication to alleviate their symptoms. With medication, many symptoms of schizophrenia disappear. If not treated with medication, this phase may last for several weeks or months. In fact, without treatment, the active phase may go on indefinitely. In very rare instances, the active phase resolves itself and symptoms disappear without treatment.

Some patients have only one episode of schizophrenia, entering the active stage only once. It is more common for patients with schizophrenia to experience multiple episodes of the disorder, with brief periods of being free of symptoms between episodes. For many patients, the active phase is characterized by positive symptoms.

Residual Stage. The final stage of schizophrenia is called the **residual stage**. The features of the residual phase are very similar to the prodromal stage. Patients in this stage do not appear psychotic but may experience some negative symptoms such as lack of emotional expression or low energy. Although patients in the residual stage do not have delusions or hallucinations, they may continue to experience strange beliefs. For example, when Kevin is in the residual stage of schizophrenia, he might still be convinced that his coworkers don't like him, even if he no longer believes that they are broadcasting a radio show about him.

PATTERNS OF ILLNESS

Schizophrenia patients may follow one of several trajectories after experiencing their first acute episode of the illness. About 35 percent of patients have an extremely severe form of the illness and experience multiple episodes interspersed with periods of increasing functional impairment. Approximately one-third of patients experience several psychotic episodes with no impairment between. About 20 percent of patients have only one psychotic episode and return to their normal level of functioning, and 10 percent have multiple episodes of schizophrenia that are followed by moderate functioning between episodes. Unfortunately, suicide is not uncommon in patients with schizophrenia. Approximately 15 percent of

patients successfully commit suicide, often because they hear a
voice telling them to do so.

THE SCHIZOPHRENIA PROGNOSIS

In summary, fewer than 20 percent of patients with a first
episode of schizophrenia have a good prognosis. That means

Pain Insensitivity and Schizophrenia

Physical pain serves a very useful purpose. When our bodies
are in pain, it signals to us that we may be sick or in danger.
Perhaps you've run the shower too hot and entered it only to
have to step back from the scorching spray. In this case, the
minor pain you feel from the hot water tells you to stand back
and turn the temperature down in order to avoid being burned.

Although many patients with schizophrenia experience
physical pain just as you do, some patients appear to have an
especially high tolerance for painful stimuli. Emil Krapelin,
the Austrian physician who was one of the first to identify what
is now known as schizophrenia, observed that "the patients
often become less sensitive to bodily discomfort; they endure
uncomfortable positions, pricks of a needle, injuries, without thinking much about it."[12] Indeed, recent observations
from physicians include case reports describing patients with
schizophrenia who experienced serious physical problems
but reported little accompanying pain. Such reports include
a patient who suffered a perforated bowel and reported
little pain and tenderness during examination, a patient who
experienced a ruptured appendix, and a patient who broke
his ankle.

that fewer than 20 out of every 100 schizophrenia patients are likely to marry, have children, and keep a job—behaviors that most consider central to having a normal, productive life. Unfortunately, the majority of people with schizophrenia experience multiple episodes of the illness. For these individuals, keeping a job and interacting with other people is

An even more intriguing observation emerged from the research of Professor Jill Hooley and her colleagues at Harvard University. Professor Hooley invited two groups of participants into her laboratory. The first group included relatives of individuals with schizophrenia. The second group included individuals who reported no family history of mental illness. The participants were asked to place a pressure algometer, a device with a small weight, onto the middle finger. The participants indicated when they first began to feel pain and removed the weight when they could no longer withstand the discomfort. Several of the relatives of schizophrenia patients reported a higher pain tolerance than the control participants with no family history of mental illness.

Thus far, researchers do not know why some individuals with schizophrenia experience less pain than people without schizophrenia. Nor do we understand why some relatives of schizophrenia patients have a higher tolerance for pain than people with no history of mental illness in their families. Some basic research suggests that some brain areas that are implicated in schizophrenia are also implicated in pain perception, although the specific association remains unclear. The relationship between pain and schizophrenia is a fascinating new avenue for research that might reveal useful information about the disorder.

often overwhelming. Approximately one-half of schizophrenia patients become so impaired that their social and occupational functioning is severely limited. These patients usually never marry, and they are unable to work or go to school. They may spend a lot of time in a psychiatric hospital or under the care of a mental health professional. All schizophrenia patients benefit from a supportive family network and an attentive treatment team.

Are there any features that indicate what course of illness a particular patient will experience? Although it is difficult to

Age or Gender?

Schizophrenia is just as common in men and women, but the severity of the disease differs between the two genders. Males, on average, suffer from more severe schizophrenic symptoms and are more seriously disabled than females. Women with schizophrenia are more likely to marry and have families and to live independently than men. At first glance, it seems there must be something about males—their physiology, their development, or their social environment—that makes them vulnerable to a more severe form of the disease. Could there be another explanation for the greater number of more seriously ill males?

Males, on average, also show their first symptoms of schizophrenia at an earlier age than females. Men typically are affected by the disease starting in their late teens or early twenties, while women are more likely to first show signs of the disease 10 years later, in their late twenties or early thirties. Perhaps early onset of the disease, not "maleness," leads to more severe illness. If this was true, males who did not develop predict with any accuracy what any one patient will experience, researchers have identified several features that appear to be associated with a poor prognosis in schizophrenia in general. Male patients who have never married, developed schizophrenia symptoms suddenly, and spend much of the first two years of their illness psychotic appear to have a more serious course of schizophrenia. Indeed, it appears that the best predictor of long-term functioning is the percentage of time a patient spent experiencing psychotic symptoms in the early years of his or her illness.[13]

the disease until their late twenties or thirties would be less disabled than men who had symptoms early, and females with early symptoms would be just as severely affected as males with early symptoms.

To answer this question, researchers have studied whether the severity of symptoms is related to age of onset, looking at males and females separately. They have found that, in fact, severity of schizophrenia is related to the age at which symptoms first appear, not specifically the gender of the patient. Both males and females with earlier onset of symptoms are more severely affected than either males or females with late onset of symptoms. Symptoms earlier in life disrupt education and development of social connections. Perhaps women with schizophrenia are more likely to marry, start careers, and have independent lives because, on average, they have 10 more years to complete their education and establish relationships before their symptoms appear. To further our understanding about schizophrenia, it is important to sort out the unique effects of age and gender on the course of the illness.

Most patients develop schizophrenia symptoms in early adulthood. The typical course of the illness, however, suggests that, by the time patients reach middle and late adulthood, psychotic symptoms are on the decline. Thus, as schizophrenia patients reach their fifties and sixties, they tend to experience fewer positive symptoms of the illness. Cognitive symptoms, however, such as problems with concentration and memory, appear to become more pronounced. Although some cognitive deterioration is common as people age, it is more severe in schizophrenia patients.

Researchers have identified three stages of schizophrenia: the prodromal stage, the acute stage, and the residual stage. The course of the illness differs among patients. Some patients experience only one episode of acute schizophrenia, whereas others cycle rapidly between episodes. Treatment with antipsychotic medications is usually necessary to alleviate schizophrenia symptoms in the acute stage. The next chapter looks at the causes of schizophrenia.

What Causes Schizophrenia?

Dr. Susan Talbot was the psychologist assigned to Kevin's case *when he and Natalie arrived at the mental health clinic. First, Dr. Talbot assessed Kevin's symptoms and learned about his recent behaviors. Kevin told her about his fear that the radio station where he was working was broadcasting information about him. Her next step involved taking a detailed family history to assemble even more information to help her formulate a diagnosis. Having Natalie there was invaluable because she was able to offer a great deal of insight.*

Natalie and Kevin are first cousins by their fathers. Kevin's father is an engineer and works for the Department of Defense. Kevin's mother is a secretary for an insurance company. Both parents are quiet people, and very kind and responsible. From the age of seven, Natalie was raised by Kevin's parents when her mother left to marry another man. Natalie's father was in and out of psychiatric hospitals, allegedly for depression and psychotic symptoms. When Natalie was 18, her father committed suicide.

Natalie, now 25, is a bright and friendly woman. She attended the University of Maryland and works as a first-grade teacher. She is close to her aunt and uncle who raised her and she feels partially responsible for helping them take care of Kevin. Kevin is also 25 years old. Although Natalie and Kevin went to the same high school, they did not share the same friends. Kevin started high school as a popular, athletic student but by the time he was a senior he had very few friends. He became obsessed with music from the 1980s, especially Morrissey, and spent a lot of time reading about the Smiths and practicing the guitar. Natalie was always kind to Kevin, and stood up for him when her friends called him a "freak." After high school, Kevin attended a local junior college and moved in with Natalie when they were both 20.

Natalie doesn't remember much about her father. Although her uncle visited him in the hospital repeatedly, he didn't feel it was an appropriate place for Natalie. Kevin never met Natalie's father and knows very little about his life. Natalie was raised to believe that her father loved her very much but was unable to express it. When he died, she felt little sadness because she knew his life was painful for him. Now she is concerned that Kevin is experiencing the same problems as her father and wants to help him.

RISK FACTORS FOR SCHIZOPHRENIA

Why do some people develop schizophrenia rather than others? **Risk factors** are the characteristics that may make a person more likely than others to develop a disorder like schizophrenia.

Schizophrenia is caused by a complex interaction between biological and environmental factors. Thus, both nature and nurture are involved in the disorder. The "nature" side has been supported by heredity studies. Indeed, ample research suggests that schizophrenia runs in families.

Family studies are conducted by identifying target individuals called **probands**. In this case, researchers study families with schizophrenia patients and determine how many family members have the disease. People with schizophrenia are much more likely to have biological relatives with schizophrenia than are people without schizophrenia. For people without schizophrenia, the likelihood that they will have a family member with the disorder is less than 1 percent, whereas approximately 10 percent of the first-degree relatives of individuals with schizophrenia also have the disorder. Three percent of second-degree relatives (first cousins), who share only 12.5 percent of their genes, also have schizophrenia.

TWIN STUDIES

Family members usually share more than genes; they share a common environment. In order to determine the impact of genes and environment, researchers must become creative in their experimental design. One way in which researchers can disentangle genes from environment is through **twin studies.** Twin studies are studies comparing the concordance for a disorder in identical (monozygotic) to fraternal (dizygotic) twins. Identical twins share 100 percent of their genes, whereas fraternal twins share only 50 percent of their genes, the same as nontwin siblings. If schizophrenia were entirely determined by genetics, we would expect all identical twins to be **concordant** for the disorder, meaning if one twin had schizophrenia the other would have it as well. It turns out that this is not the case. Although the concordance rates are significantly higher for identical twins compared to fraternal twins, far less than 100 percent of identical twins with schizophrenia are concordant for the disorder. If a member of an identical twin pair has schizophrenia, his or her twin has a 28 percent chance of also having the disease. In contrast, if a member of a fraternal twin pair has schizophrenia, his twin has only a 6 percent chance of also having the disease. This suggests a very significant nongenetic (or environmental) influence on the development of schizophrenia.

ADOPTION STUDIES

Why are some twin pairs concordant for schizophrenia whereas others are not? There must be factors other than genes that contribute to the development of schizophrenia. Another creative way of studying heredity is through **adoption studies.**

One of the first large adoption studies was the Heston Study in 1966. Heston identified 47 adopted children whose biological mothers had schizophrenia. He compared these children to a group of children from the same foster homes whose biological mothers did not have schizophrenia. Heston found that 16.6 percent of the children of schizophrenic mothers became schizophrenic as adults, compared to none of the

The Genain Quadruplets

Perhaps one of the most remarkable examples of the complex interaction of genes and environment in schizophrenia is the case of the Genain Quadruplets. The Genain Quadruplets, four identical twin girls born in 1930, became a focus of clinical interest in the 1960s when each sister was diagnosed with schizophrenia. Genain, a fictitious name used in order to protect the family's identity, comes from the Greek term meaning "dire birth." The fictitious names of the girls, Nora, Iris, Myra, and Hester, were chosen to mimic the four letters in NIMH, the National Institute of Mental Health.

Although one might conclude that the Genains are evidence of the hereditary nature of schizophrenia, the fact that each girl's illness was unique in its symptoms, severity, course, and outcome confirms that environmental factors are integral to the disorder's development. Nora, the firstborn, while identified as the brightest of the four girls, was hospitalized at 22 and never lived independently for an extended period of time. Iris, the second sister, spent 12 years in a psychiatric hospital starting at the age of 22. Myra, the third sister, is the only one to marry and have children. It is not certain whether she has schizoaffective control children. Thus, even though none of the children were raised by schizophrenic parents, the children who had schizophrenia in their biological families were more likely to develop the disorder.

Another large adoption study is the Danish study by Kenneth Kendler and colleagues that began in the 1980s. Kendler identified adults with schizophrenia who had been adopted when they

disorder or schizophrenia, and she did not experience delusions or hallucinations until she was in her forties. Hester, the youngest sister, is the most severely ill. She was taken out of school in the eleventh grade and never worked outside the home.

Dr. David Rosenthal and the staff at the National Institute of Mental Health spent many years following this family. In addition to the girls, many family members had some form of mental illness. Mr. Genain, the father of the girls, was paranoid and most likely an alcoholic. He was frequently unemployed and was irritable and withdrawn. He was concerned that the girls would be raped unless he kept them at home. Investigators at the NIMH believed that Mr. Genain himself raped at least two of the girls, despite his concern for their innocence. Mrs. Genain did not appear to interfere on behalf of her daughters and protect them from the real threat of their father. Mrs. Genain's mother, the girls' grandmother, appeared to have suffered some form of a "breakdown" and experienced what investigators believed to be paranoid schizophrenia. The four sisters were dealt a double blow, a genetic predisposition to schizophrenia from both sides of the family, and a family environment that was cruel and stressful.

were infants and compared them to other adoptees who did not have schizophrenia. He found that 13.3 percent of the biological relatives of the schizophrenic adoptees had schizophrenia disorders, compared to 1.3 percent of the relatives of the healthy adoptees. This may be interpreted as even more evidence for a biological component of schizophrenia.

What factors in the environment increase the likelihood that schizophrenia will develop? In 1997 Dr. Karl-Erik Wahlberg and colleagues of the University of Oulu in Finland studied the qualities of the adoptive family to help determine why some children with a biological family history of schizophrenia developed the disorder while others did not. Wahlberg was interested in the way in which adoptive families communicated with one another and studied **communication deviance**. Family members who use speech that is unclear and difficult to follow are considered to be high in communication deviance. In the Finnish adoption study, biological children of schizophrenic mothers who were raised in adoptive families with high communication deviance were more likely to become schizophrenic than children raised in families with low communication deviance. This evidence suggests that the combination of genes and a stressful family environment makes schizophrenia more likely.

PRENATAL ENVIRONMENT

When we think of a child's "environment," we tend to think of their family and friends. In fact, our first "environment" is inside the womb. The nine months during which a baby develops inside the mother lay important groundwork for healthy development after birth. Researchers have found that there are qualities of the prenatal environment that may increase the likelihood that someone will develop schizophrenia. For example, research has shown that patients with schizophrenia are much more likely to be born following a complicated pregnancy or delivery. Additionally, schizophrenia patients are more likely to be born during winter months. There are two ways in which the prenatal environment may affect an infant with a genetic propensity for schizophrenia.

In 1957, there was an influenza epidemic in Helsinki, Finland. Sarnoff Mednick at the University of Southern California wanted to know if mothers who had the flu while they were pregnant were more likely to have children who later developed schizophrenia. Indeed, Mednick found that children who were born to mothers who had the flu in the second trimester were more likely to have schizophrenia as adults. Although researchers are still uncertain as to how exactly the influenza virus affects the unborn child, one hypothesis is that maternal antibodies cross the placental barrier and disrupt brain development.

Children whose mothers are malnourished may also be more likely to develop schizophrenia as adults. The Dutch Hunger Winter was a period of extreme famine in the Netherlands. In 1944, a Nazi blockade prevented many Dutch citizens from getting enough food for their families. Many people became very sick and some died from starvation. Research has shown that the children who were conceived at the height of the famine were twice as likely to develop schizophrenia as children who were conceived at other times. Fetal malnutrition may play a role in the development of schizophrenia.

BRAIN DIFFERENCES

In the past, researchers could only examine the brain after a patient died. Now, there is technology that allows researchers to examine the brains of living people. New techniques, including magnetic resonance imaging (MRI), are rapidly advancing our knowledge about the brain and schizophrenia. Still, there are several challenges to studying brain structure and function in relation to a major mental illness. One such challenge includes

Schizophrenia and prenatal exposure to flu

A new study adds more evidence to research suggesting that prenatal exposure to influenza early in a pregnacy, increases the risk of schizophrenia in the child.

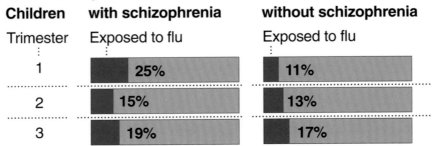

Children   with schizophrenia   without schizophrenia

Trimester	Exposed to flu	Exposed to flu
1	25%	11%
2	15%	13%
3	19%	17%

Of 189 women in the study, 64 had children who developed schizophrenia. 20 women were tested in the first trimester with five (25%) exposed to influenza.

SOURCE: Archives of General Psychiatry   AP

Figure 4.1 This graphic shows the results of a 2004 study examining the risk of schizophrenia for children with prenatal exposure to influenza. © *AP Images*

figuring out whether differences in the brain were present before the illness and thus part of the cause, or if they are the result of symptoms. In addition, most schizophrenia patients take medication, which may also play a role in changing the way the brain looks and works. There are many diseases that affect the brain and may cause or result from brain abnormalities. All the brain differences you will read about can also be found in individuals without schizophrenia. This means that, to date, there are no brain abnormalities that specifically distinguish schizophrenia patients from normal, healthy people.

Deep within the brain are fluid-filled spaces called **ventricles**. Several studies have shown that relative to individuals without schizophrenia, schizophrenia patients have enlarged ventricles. If one's ventricles are large compared to what is

Famine damage

A study of famine in China found children born to severely malnourished women are more likely to develop schizophrenia, results that are nearly identical to a study of famine in Holland.

Percent risk for schizophrenia in Wuhu and surrounding counties, 1956-1965

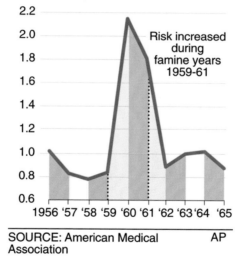

SOURCE: American Medical Association   AP

Figure 4.2 This graphic depicts a study of famine in China, which found that children born to severely malnourished women are more likely to develop schizophrenia. © *AP Images*

normal for a brain of a particular size, that means that there is less functional brain tissue. Enlarged ventricles are not unique to schizophrenia and are associated with several other disorders of the brain, including Alzheimer's disease and chronic alcohol use. Other studies using MRI support the theory that schizophrenia patients have less working brain tissue. Studies have shown that there is a 3 percent reduction in brain volume in schizophrenia patients relative to normal, healthy study participants. This lower brain volume has been identified early in the schizophrenic illness, thus suggesting that this general brain abnormality may come before the illness rather than resulting from repeated psychotic episodes or medication taken to treat symptoms of schizophrenia.

Although several parts of the brain have been found to be different in schizophrenia patients, two areas have received the most clinical attention. The first are the frontal lobes of the brain, which are the areas directly behind the forehead that are responsible for planning and problem solving. This area is among the last to completely mature in normal individuals. Problems in frontal lobe functioning may appear as difficulties in concentration and attention. Many schizophrenia patients appear to have these problems. One task by which researchers can study frontal lobe function is called the **Wisconsin Card Sort Test** (WCST). In the WCST, participants are asked to look at cards and sort them according to color, shape, or number. The test administrator will not tell the participant the rule by which they should sort but will tell the participant if they are sorting correctly. Someone without frontal lobe damage will try to sort according to one rule, perhaps number, but will change to shape or color until the administrator tells them they are correct. After the participant sorts a few cards, the test administrator changes the rule and now the participant must try to figure out the new rule. Most people have no problem with this task. They will change from number to color or shape until the administrator tells them they are correct. But for someone with schizophrenia or another form of frontal lobe damage, the rule change can present a real challenge. These patients might keep sorting the cards according to the old rule, a process called **perseveration**.

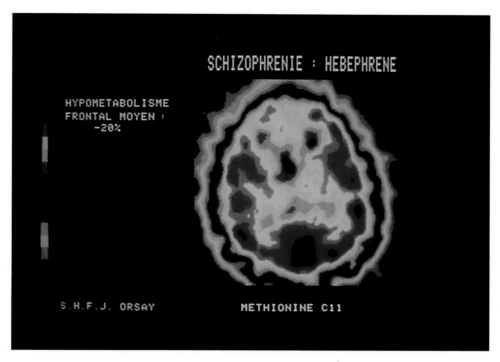

SCHIZOPHRENIE : HEBEPHRENE

HYPOMETABOLISME
FRONTAL MOYEN :
-20%

S.H.F.J. ORSAY   METHIONINE C11

Figure 4.3 This colored PET scan shows the axial section of the brain of a person suffering from schizophrenia, with areas in red indicating protein synthesis. More red areas of protein synthesis would be expected in the frontal lobes of the brain (top). © *CNRI/Photo Researchers, Inc.*

Even after being told repeatedly that they are wrong, they are unable to figure out that there is a new rule in place. When researchers study brain activity while a patient is participating in the WCST, they find that there is decreased activity in the frontal lobes in patients with schizophrenia relative to normal, healthy participants.

Another part of the brain that may be implicated in schizophrenia is the **thalamus.** The thalamus is a small, oblong collection of sensory and motor processing areas in the center of the brain. Commonly considered a major relay center of the brain, the thalamus receives most of the information collected from our environment via sensory organs (eyes, ears, skin) and makes connections with areas of the cortex and brainstem. The circuitry that connects the thalamus with other brain areas, including the frontal lobes and the cerebellum, may be impaired in patients with schizophrenia. Indeed, some preliminary research by Nancy Andreasen at the University of Iowa suggests that these thalamic pathways may be implicated in a number of schizophrenic symptoms.[14]

SCHIZOPHRENIA AND NEUROTRANSMITTERS

When scientists study how the brains of people with mental illness are different, they are commonly interested in two issues: brain *structure* and *function.* Researchers can study structure by comparing the brain anatomy in people with schizophrenia to brain anatomy in people without schizophrenia. Ventricle size is a good example of a *structural* anatomical difference seen in schizophrenia, whereas frontal lobe activity is a good example of a *functional* anatomical difference seen in schizophrenia. Another area of interest to researchers is communication within the brain. Studying communication in the brain, a process carried out by substances called **neurotransmitters**, can help reveal even more about how the brains of people with schizophrenia differ from the brains of people without it. Studying neurotransmitters can reveal both structural and functional differences in the schizophrenic brain. Next, we will discuss how neurotransmitters work and how they appear to be implicated in schizophrenia symptoms.

Neurotransmitters. Neurotransmitters are effectively the "messengers" of the brain, carrying information from one brain cell to another. Brain cells, called **neurons**, are responsive to different kinds of neurotransmitters and have receptors built specifically for them. Neurons that are sensitive to specific

Figure 4.4 This computer graphic of a synapse shows the release of neurotransmitters (pink spheres at lower center) by vesicles inside the synaptic knob (upper center). The neurotransmitters will cross the gap and bond to the receptors of the adjacent cell, which is how information is transmitted along the nervous system. © *Alfred Pasieka/Photo Researchers, Inc.*

neurotransmitters tend to cluster together, creating circuits in the brain for processing specific kinds of information.

Neurotransmitters are released from a neuron when it signals another brain cell. The neurotransmitters are released into the small space between the two neurons, called the **synapse**. In the synapse, the neurotransmitters attach, or bind, to the receptors at the ends of another neuron, thus affecting the activity of the new neuron. The new neuron takes in as much of the neurotransmitter as it can and then releases the excess back into the synapse. The excess is reabsorbed by the first neuron, a process known as **reuptake**. Drugs that treat mood disorders like depression (e.g. Prozac, Zoloft) regulate the amount of certain neurotransmitters available in the brain and the process of neurotransmitter reuptake, and affect communication between brain cells.

There are many different neurotransmitters in the brain. Two that have been found to be involved in schizophrenia symptoms are **dopamine** and **glutamate**. Dopamine is primarily involved in movement and thoughts. Dopamine has also been associated with novelty seeking, or interest in new experiences and reward. Some illegal drugs, such as cocaine and methamphetamine, work by affecting dopamine function in the brain. Thus, dopamine is associated with feelings of pleasure and well-being. Dopamine pathways in the brain are highly specialized and may influence different kinds of thinking or behavior. People with high levels of dopamine in certain parts of the brain may also experience psychotic symptoms or paranoid thinking, symptoms of schizophrenia.

Due to several lines of converging evidence, many scientists believe that dopamine is the cause of many schizophrenic symptoms. The "dopamine hypothesis" dates from the 1960s and emerged from three important observations. In 1952, a drug called clorpromazine was first used to treat schizophrenia.

It worked by blocking dopamine receptors and was successful in treating many schizophrenia patients. A second observation involved the effects of amphetamines. Amphetamines work by making the brain think that there is too much dopamine in the system. People who abuse amphetamines often experience schizophrenia-like symptoms, primarily paranoia and auditory hallucinations. Parkinson's disease is a disease in which patients experience physical movement problems. Patients with Parkinson's are treated with a drug that effectively increases the level of dopamine in the brain. This drug, called L-DOPA, has been associated with complications or side effects that look a lot like schizophrenic symptoms. Patients treated with L-DOPA sometimes experience psychotic symptoms, which provide researchers with more evidence that high levels of dopamine in some parts of the brain are implicated in schizophrenia.

When the brain perceives that there is an excess of dopamine, schizophrenic-like symptoms appear. We still don't know what causes this excess of dopamine. Do some people produce too much dopamine? Is the breakdown of dopamine somehow inhibited in some people? Or do some people have dopamine receptors that are especially sensitive so their brain thinks that there is extra dopamine even when there isn't? These are questions that have yet to be answered definitively.

One problem in studying dopamine in schizophrenia is that we can only directly study the presence of dopamine in autopsies. Presently, we can study the **metabolite** of dopamine, the substance that remains in the body after dopamine is used. The metabolite of dopamine, HVA, can be found and measured in our **cerebrospinal fluid**, which is the fluid we have in our spinal column and in the ventricles of our brain. In order to measure this fluid, patients must endure a spinal tap, which requires the insertion of a long needle into the spine to access the fluid. This is a painful procedure, and there are risks of infection and complications. Because of these risks, few people are willing to undergo this procedure to be part of an experimental study.

As yet, there is little evidence that people with schizophrenia are producing more dopamine than are people without schizophrenia. Instead, there is some evidence that people with schizophrenia are extremely sensitive to dopamine. Through postmortem studies, researchers have discovered that relative to people without schizophrenia, schizophrenic patients have more receptors for dopamine. Although this evidence is promising, it is unclear whether schizophrenia is caused by an excess of dopamine receptors, or whether the excess of receptors is caused by the illness or treatment.

Another neurotransmitter that may play an important role in schizophrenia is glutamate. Glutamate is believed to have an important role in learning and the formation and encoding of memory. Some hallucinogenic drugs, such as PCP, are known to block glutamate receptors. Like amphetamines, PCP can cause paranoia that mimics schizophrenic symptoms. When people with schizophrenia take PCP, it often makes their symptoms worse. In autopsy studies, lower levels of glutamate have been found in the brains of schizophrenic patients. Dr. Daniel Weinberger, an influential researcher of schizophrenia at the National Institute of Mental Health, has suggested that an interaction between dopamine and glutamate is at the core of schizophrenia. Dopamine receptors also reduce the action of glutamate. If there are too many dopamine receptors, glutamate's effects will be blocked.

Studying how neurotransmitters work is especially challenging. However, these investigations can provide crucial information about what causes schizophrenia and how best to treat it.

FAMILY ENVIRONMENT

Although early schizophrenia researchers such as Bleuler and Kraepelin insisted that schizophrenia is, at its core, a disease caused by biological factors, many others believed that schizophrenia was caused by the family. Today, we know that no family can, by itself, "cause" schizophrenia. Research suggests, however, that the family environment does play an important role in a patient's treatment. Some families may have qualities that increase the likelihood that a patient will **relapse** and experience another schizophrenic episode.

In the early 1900s, psychologists created the term "schizophrenigenic mother" to describe the cold, distant mothers of patients with schizophrenia. Before we had a good understanding of how the brain works, many therapists blamed family members for their schizophrenic children. This must have caused family members extreme stress. Not only did they have to live with a psychotic child, but also they had to suffer the guilt of being seen as the cause of the illness.

When schizophrenia patients leave the hospital and return to their homes, some fare better than others. Researchers became interested in figuring out why some patients relapse whereas others do not. Clinicians and researchers believed that there might be qualities of the family that protect the patient from relapse and other qualities that increase the likelihood that the patient will experience another episode.

As previously mentioned, a family's communication deviance—vague and confusing speech—is a risk factor in schizophrenia. Another measure of the communication of family members is called **expressed emotion**. Expressed emotion, or EE, is a measure of the negative communication directed at a patient by family members. EE consists of three parts: criticism, hostility, and emotional overinvolvement. A family member who expresses criticism is expressing disapproval or dislike of the patient. Hostility is a more extreme form of criticism that involves a rejection of the patient. **Emotional overinvolvement** involves dramatic, overconcerned behaviors directed toward the patient. For example, when questioned about her schizophrenic son, an emotionally overinvolved mother might respond, "When he spends all day in bed, I just feel terrible. I wish he knew how hard it was on me. Sometimes I lock him out of his room when he gets up to go to the bathroom. I just have to force him to get out and do something." Not only does this mother emphasize how her son's illness makes *her* feel, but also she forcibly locks him out of his room. In 1998, Ron Butzlaff and Jill Hooley at Harvard University found that patients living in a high EE home environment were more than twice as likely to relapse in the first year following a hospitalization compared with patients returning to a low EE home. The good news is that EE can be lowered with family therapy. When EE levels are lowered, relapse rates are reduced.

Why might the way a family communicates affect a patient's recovery? Current understanding suggests that high EE or communication deviance creates a stressful environment for schizophrenic patients. When we are stressed, a substance called **cortisol** is released in the brain. Cortisol has been found to trigger dopamine activity and to affect glutamate release. According to this theory, a stressful environment can directly affect the chemicals in the brain that are implicated in schizophrenic symptoms.

SOCIAL CLASS

Schizophrenia is found at all socioeconomic levels. The lower the socioeconomic level, however, the more likely you are to find someone with schizophrenia. The **sociogenic hypothesis** holds that because living in poverty is more stressful, one's risk for developing schizophrenia is increased. One can imagine that relative to a mother with more resources, an impoverished pregnant woman is less likely to receive adequate prenatal care, is more likely to be exposed to viruses, and is more likely to experience a complicated delivery. All three of these are risk factors of schizophrenia. Alternatively, the **social drift hypothesis**, also known as "downward drift," suggests that people with schizophrenia drift down the socioeconomic ladder because of their social and occupational impairment. So which is true? Research shows that more cases of schizophrenia develop in families of lower socioeconomic status, but patients also drift downward because of their illness. Thus, both the sociogenic and the social drift hypotheses correctly predict schizophrenia.

Some of the risk factors of schizophrenia include a family history of schizophrenia, qualities of the prenatal environment, and family communication patterns. The next chapter discusses how clinicians treat schizophrenia.

5 Treatment and Outcome

Dr. Talbot is fairly certain that Kevin meets the diagnostic criteria *for schizophrenia. His hallucinations and delusions are evidence that he is experiencing psychotic behavior. Dr. Talbot believes that his behavior change in high school, from being a popular student to becoming reclusive, was the first indication of the illness. At 25, Kevin is just about at the average age for the first episode of schizophrenia. Kevin's cousin Natalie has given Dr. Talbot even more evidence that Kevin is schizophrenic. Her father, Kevin's uncle, was hospitalized for psychiatric symptoms that sound a lot like schizophrenia.*

In order to provide the most comprehensive treatment, Dr. Talbot assembles a team of clinicians. She assigns Kevin to a psychiatrist who will prescribe and monitor his medications. She also introduces Kevin to a case manager who will help figure out whether Kevin needs financial or housing assistance. For the next few weeks, Kevin will be in the hospital and will attend group meetings as well as individual meetings with Dr. Talbot. In the group meetings, Kevin will learn more about schizophrenia and how to avoid relapse. Individual psychotherapy will give Kevin an opportunity to talk about his personal experience with schizophrenia and learn how to live with the illness. All the clinicians—Dr. Talbot, the psychiatrist, the case manager, and the psychologist—will meet regularly to discuss Kevin's treatment and progress. Dr. Talbot will offer Natalie and the rest of Kevin's family information

*about schizophrenia and suggest support groups where they can
learn more about living with someone who suffers from the illness.
Having an experienced, supportive treatment team in place is the
best assurance that Kevin will recover as quickly and completely
as possible.*

HISTORY OF TREATMENT

Before prescription medications, treatment for schizophrenia
was primitive at best. Patients who lacked financial resources
were usually confined to asylums and often treated with inhu-
mane and degrading methods. Patients with schizophrenia
were sometimes bound in straitjackets or subjected to radical
brain surgery. Some patients were treated with **fever therapy** in
which high fevers were induced in an attempt to alleviate psychotic symptoms. Others were subjected to **electroconvulsive
therapy** (ECT) or simply tied to their beds. Although patients
who came from wealthy families were able to obtain more
humane treatment in private hospitals, treatment options
were few until the introduction of antipsychotic medication
in the 1950s.

TYPICAL ANTIPSYCHOTIC MEDICATION

The first medications designed to treat schizophrenia are now
called **typical antipsychotic medications,** or first-generation
antipsychotics. Many of these early medications are still used
today, and are helpful for many patients. Some examples of
these medications are chlorpromazine and **haloperidol.** Typical
antipsychotic medications work by blocking the effects of
dopamine. Because of this primary function, some call these
medications **neuroleptics,** which literally means "seizing the
neuron." Typical antipsychotic medications are most effective
in treating positive symptoms such as hallucinations and delusions. Although some patients may improve after only a week

Figure 5.1 Treatment of people with schizophrenia before medication was available was primitive at best. Some were bound in straightjackets, such as the one shown on this patient in the Ohio Insane Asylum, 1946. © *Jerry Cooke/Photo Researchers, Inc.*

or two of treatment, the most complete effects of these medications are usually seen after six to eight weeks. Unfortunately, treatment with typical antipsychotic medications does cause some uncomfortable side effects. Many patients experience significant weight gain, drowsiness, or dry mouth. Some patients experience **extra-pyramidal side effects** (EPS), which are uncontrollable bodily movements such as muscle spasms or shaking. Other medications can be used to minimize extra-pyramidal side effects, although the relief is only temporary. In fact, studies have shown that patients who take typical antipsychotic medications for 10 years or more may develop a serious condition called **tardive dyskinesia** in which patients experience involuntary movements of the tongue, lips, and neck. Tardive dyskinesia is very uncomfortable and can be embarrassing to many patients.

ATYPICAL ANTIPSYCHOTIC MEDICATION

Although the typical antipsychotic medications are effective in treating positive symptoms, they are relatively unsuccessful in treating negative symptoms. Additionally, these medications cause unpleasant side effects. In the 1980s, researchers focused on developing medications that treated more aspects of schizophrenia and did so without disabling side effects. These medications that are used frequently today are called **atypical antipsychotic medications**, or second-generation antipsychotics.

Clozapine was the first atypical antipsychotic and was designed to help patients who did not respond well to traditional neuroleptics. It became available in the United States in 1989 and now is prescribed widely by psychiatrists. Newer atypical antipsychotic medications include risperidone and olanzapine. These medications provide relief for patients without the uncomfortable side effects. Unlike early antipsychotic medications, atypical antipsychotic medications are effective at treating both positive and negative symptoms.

How do these medications differ from earlier medications? Researchers speculate that traditional antipsychotic medications completely block one kind of dopamine receptor, leaving other types of dopamine receptors unaffected. Atypical antipsychotics

John Hinckley Jr.

John Hinckley Jr. was, by all accounts, a normal child. Born to successful and wealthy parents, John was the youngest of three children. His mother doted on him and remembers him being quiet and introspective. In high school, John spent most of his time alone in his room, playing his guitar and listening to the Beatles. Although his parents attributed his isolation to shyness, high school classmates recall that he was odd and a loner.

After high school, John completed a year of college in Texas before dropping out to pursue his dream of becoming a songwriter. He moved to Hollywood, found an apartment, and worked on his music. While in California, he watched the movie *Taxi Driver* more than 15 times. He became obsessed with the story of an American recluse who stalks a political candidate.

In 1979, John Hinckley bought his first gun, which was to become part of a collection. Personal photographs reveal him holding a gun to his temple on two occasions. According to later reports, John played Russian roulette twice shortly after he acquired his first handgun. By 1980, John was experiencing more symptoms of mental illness. He began treatment with antidepressants and tranquilizers. Despite his psychiatric problems, John continued to add to his gun collection.

In May of 1980, John Hinckley read an article in *People* magazine about the actress Jodie Foster. In the article, he learned that the actress was enrolled at Yale. Hinckley was impressed by Foster because of her role in *Taxi Driver*. He decided to enroll in a writing course at Yale so that he could be close to her. While there, John tried to establish a relationship with the actress. He wrote her letters and poems and left them for her in her mailbox. Because his

Figure 5.2 Would-be assassin John Hinckley is wrestled to the ground after his attempt on President Reagan's life. © *Ron Edmonds/AP*

attempts at making contact with her were largely unsuccessful, he decided to try something different to get her attention. John Hinckley believed that by assassinating the president, he could obtain Jodie Foster's love and devotion. On Monday, March 30, 1981, John wrote a letter to Jodie Foster describing his plan to assassinate President Reagan. He went to Washington, D.C., and checked into a hotel. In the afternoon, he left his hotel room and took a cab to the Washington Hilton, where President Ronald Reagan was to speak to a labor convention.

(continues)

(continued)

At 1:30 P.M., John fired six shots. The bullets from Hinckley's gun struck Ronald Reagan in the chest, Reagan press secretary James Brady in the temple, police officer Thomas Delahanty in the neck, and Secret Service agent Timothy J. McCarthy in the stomach. Hinckley was immediately arrested and was tried for his crime a year later. On June 21, 1982, after seven weeks of testimony and three days of deliberation by the jury, John Hinckley was found not guilty by reason of insanity. He currently lives at St. Elizabeth's Hospital in Washington, D.C., where he is treated for schizophrenia.

appear to block many kinds of dopamine receptors less completely. This may help alleviate all types of schizophrenia symptoms but not cause the movement disorders associated with typical medications.

Unfortunately, there are side effects associated with atypical antipsychotic medications. Like the earlier medications, atypical medications can cause drowsiness and weight gain. In very rare cases, clozapine can cause a blood disorder called **agranulocytosis.** In order to prevent this condition, patients taking clozapine must take weekly blood tests to monitor their blood count.

PSYCHOLOGICAL TREATMENTS

Many patients must try a variety of medications before finding one that controls their symptoms. This can be a very difficult and frustrating process. Many months or years may pass before a patient begins to get relief from his or her symptoms and accept the medication's side effects. To help make this process easier, many people with schizophrenia benefit from therapy, family support, a community-based rehabilitation program, or some combination of the three. Psychological treatments include individual psychotherapy, cognitive behavioral therapy, and social skills training.

INDIVIDUAL PSYCHOTHERAPY

Sigmund Freud created **psychoanalysis**, a philosophy in which symptoms of mental illness are considered external expressions of unconscious problems. In psychoanalysis, an analyst and patient meet frequently to reveal and explore these unconscious conflicts. Psychoanalysis is hard work for both patient and therapist. In the first half of the twentieth century, patients with schizophrenia were routinely treated with psychoanalysis. Psychotic patients were asked to discuss their symptoms and consider them in relation to their childhood experience—an exhausting and potentially impossible task. In the 1980s, researchers began to reveal that not only was psychoanalysis not helpful for patients with schizophrenia, but also, in some cases, it actually made people worse. Researchers suspect that the stress of a psychoanalytic session was simply too much for many patients with schizophrenia to handle.

More recently, therapists have begun to use **personal therapy** to treat schizophrenia. Personal therapy is another form of individual psychotherapy in which patients work one-on-one with a therapist to learn coping and life skills. Different skills are taught at appropriate stages of a patient's recovery. For example, when a patient is just coming home from the hospital, a therapy session might focus on identifying and managing stress. Later, a patient might learn how to talk about a problem with a family member.

COGNITIVE BEHAVIORAL THERAPY

Many mental disorders are characterized by thoughts and behaviors that make people unhappy or uncomfortable. People

Figure 5.3 Sigmund Freud created psychoanalysis, an ineffective treatment for schizophrenia. *National Library of Medicine*

who are depressed often think negatively about themselves and believe that they are worthless. As you have learned, many schizophrenia patients experience delusions, or false beliefs that are resistant to change. The goal of cognitive behavioral therapy (CBT) is to change these maladaptive thoughts and behaviors. In the past, CBT was used primarily to treat depression and anxiety disorders. Clinicians thought schizophrenic patients were too impaired to be treated with CBT. Recently, researchers in the United Kingdom have explored the use of CBT with schizophrenia patients. Therapists challenge the reality of hallucinations and delusions and ask patients to consider alternative explanations for their strange experiences. The goal of this process is to decrease the impact of symptoms, keep patients out of the hospital, and improve their social interactions. Because this is such a new treatment for schizophrenia, there is little research to tell us how helpful it is. One study has shown that schizophrenia patients who undergo CBT report that their symptoms improve. Studies have also found, however, that other types of therapy are equally effective. Researchers wonder whether the type of therapy is less important than the emotional support therapy in general provides.

SOCIAL SKILLS TRAINING

Patients with schizophrenia often have very poor interpersonal skills.[15] Making appropriate eye contact, controlling the volume of their voice, and participating in a conversation can all be difficult for them. The goal of social skills training is to teach patients basic life skills, including how to interact with other people. A typical social skills training class might focus on only one feature of social interaction, like how to make good eye contact. Patients will learn about appropriate eye contact, practice using role play, and receive feedback from a therapist. After the lesson, patients will be asked to use this new skill in the real world and talk in the next session about how it worked. Social skills training can also help patients learn a variety of basic skills, including taking care of basic hygiene, preparing meals, and managing their money. Classes might include basic cooking lessons, fire safety, or how to write a check. As you can see, social skills training is very different from psychotherapy. Indeed, Michael Green at the University of California, Los Angeles, has noted that social skills training is like taking dance lessons: It is a practical, hands-on process.

Does social skills training work? Alex Kopelowicz at the University of California, Los Angeles, found that patients improved with social skills training. Other studies, however, have found that patients improve very little, if at all. Some critics of social skills training suggest that patients have a hard time taking what they learn in a class and applying it to their real lives. Perhaps some of the memory or attention problems that schizophrenia patients experience make learning new skills difficult. In order to address this issue, researchers are now focusing on developing methods to help patients improve their learning skills.

FAMILY THERAPY

Dealing with a family member with a serious mental illness can be difficult. In order to make the transition from hospital to home as smooth as possible, many schizophrenia patients attend therapy with their families. Some family members may also attend their own support groups where they can talk with other people who are living with someone with schizophrenia. Education about the illness is crucial for both patient and family member. Learning how to identify changes in the patient, how to communicate with the patient, and how to be supportive to the patient are all skills that can be taught in family therapy. You have learned that schizophrenia patients who return to a high expressed emotion (EE) home are more likely to relapse than are patients who return to a low expressed emotion home

(Chapter 4). For this reason, support for relatives of schizophrenia patients can be helpful for patients with schizophrenia and their family members.

CASE MANAGEMENT

Schizophrenia affects all areas of people's lives, including where they live, who they live with, and how they pay their bills. For someone who is learning to live with mental illness, these simple tasks can become daunting, if not impossible. An important part of treatment for schizophrenia involves providing a support person to help with all these basic needs. A case manager is someone who helps schizophrenia patients with housing, social support, and treatment.

Case managers are experts on community resources. They are familiar with housing options for people with mental illness and can refer homeless patients to shelters, halfway houses, and residential treatment programs. Many schizophrenia patients need to apply for government support such as Social Security Disability Income. A case manager can help provide and complete the necessary paperwork so that a patient is able to receive financial support. Case managers become an essential part of treatment once a patient has left the hospital. Patients are encouraged to check in with their case manager, who, in turn, monitors the patient's treatment and progress.

PREVENTING RELAPSE

People with schizophrenia are encouraged to follow some basic advice in order to manage their illness and avoid relapse. Some therapists suggest that patients keep records of their daily behavior so that they might become aware of significant behavioral changes. Major changes in behavior could be a **warning sign** of future relapse. Many patients learn to identify their personal warning signs and keep a record of them. If patients notice a change in their behavior, they are asked to contact their therapists as soon as possible to determine whether they need some change in treatment. With luck and good timing, treatment can be modified to help the patient feel better.

Maintaining a healthy lifestyle is important for everyone, but especially so for schizophrenia patients. Medication management, taking the proper dose at the same time each day, is crucial. To help patients remember when to take their medication, some use pill boxes with each daily dose in a separate compartment. This helps them to know when they should take a dose of medication and when they need to take another.

Drugs and alcohol are particularly dangerous for people with mental illness. Caffeine and nicotine, the addictive and mind-altering substances in coffee and cigarettes, respectively, should only be used in moderation by people with schizophrenia. People with schizophrenia might be especially sensitive to the effects of these substances. Getting an appropriate amount of sleep can be helpful in preventing relapse. Research suggests that sleep can affect mood. When patients are getting too much sleep, it could be a sign of depression. Too little sleep may signify anxiety or mania. To this end, patients are encouraged to structure their day and record their activities. They might rise at the same time each morning and follow a daily routine, ending their day at the same time every night. When a patient follows a routine, it is easier to monitor behavior changes. This way, patients can recognize when they are sleeping more or less than usual.

Avoiding stress in general is a good rule of thumb for schizophrenia patients. Measures one can take to avoid stress include surrounding oneself with supportive people, avoiding overstimulating movies or TV programs, and following a simple routine. New experiences, although exciting for most, can be especially stressful for people with schizophrenia. When schizophrenia patients take their medication, maintain a healthy lifestyle, keep a routine, monitor stress, and check in with their treatment team regularly, they are more likely to successfully manage their illness.

OUTCOME

In 1994, a study published in the *American Journal of Psychiatry* examined existing data to figure out just how likely patients are to recover from schizophrenia. The researchers studied outcome data from more than 100 years for patients treated around the world. Not surprisingly, after the creation of antipsychotic medications, outcome for schizophrenia was much improved. With medication, patients are far more likely to live independently and get relief from their symptoms. Outcomes appeared to worsen in the years 1986–1991. This is because the diagnostic criteria changed in 1980 and it became much more difficult for someone to be diagnosed with the illness. Before 1980, patients who today would be diagnosed with major depression might have been diagnosed with schizophrenia instead. The effect of this change is that patients who were treated for schizophrenia had a more severe form of the illness after 1980 and thus were harder to treat successfully.

So what percentage of patients with schizophrenia has a positive treatment outcome? Another recent study suggests that from 15 to 25 years after developing schizophrenia, approximately 38 percent of patients have a fairly good outcome and will be able to function reasonably well after treatment. It is unusual that a patient with schizophrenia returns to his or her level of functioning before developing the illness, but many are able to successfully manage their symptoms with medication and therapy. At the opposite extreme, about 12 percent of patients require long-term psychiatric hospitalization.[16]

There are several forms of treatment for individuals with schizophrenia. Antipsychotic medications have been used for many years and successfully reduce symptoms. Newer drugs, called atypical antipsychotic medications, are providing new hope for patients whose symptoms were resistant to traditional neuroleptics. Different types of counseling can help patients with schizophrenia learn to manage stress, monitor their symptoms, and master basic life skills. Family members are supported by family therapy, where they learn about their relative's illness and have an opportunity to talk about the challenges of living with a mentally ill family member. Case managers help patients make the transition from hospital to community. Treatment for schizophrenia has improved drastically over the past 100 years. Patients now have a much better chance of living independently and managing their illness.

Impact on Families and Society

Kevin has been in the hospital for six weeks and has improved significantly. *The voices are not bothering him anymore and he no longer believes that his coworkers dislike him. Kevin is taking risperidone, an atypical antipsychotic medication that can effectively reduce symptoms without too many side effects. Kevin is tolerating the medicine well, and he feels like it is helping him. He has gained a bit of weight, but he is exercising daily in the gym on the hospital unit and trying to eat healthy foods. All in all, Kevin is functioning fairly well.*

Dr. Talbot has enjoyed working with Kevin. A few weeks after he was admitted to the hospital, Kevin's sense of humor emerged in their sessions together. He started to laugh and talk freely about how he has been feeling and how he hopes to control his symptoms. Dr. Talbot is pleased to see Kevin's personality return to normal. His emotional responses to events, rather than being blunted or absent, are now appropriate. Kevin is extremely grateful to Natalie but also feels guilty about causing her stress. He remembers accusing his coworkers of broadcasting a radio show about him and is too embarrassed to return to work right away. Dr. Talbot is helping Kevin determine the best option for him after he leaves the hospital—to return to the apartment he shared with Natalie, or to find a place on his own.

Dr. Talbot has also met with Natalie on two occasions. Natalie is very concerned about Kevin. She doesn't know how she can help him and isn't sure whether she wants to live with him again. Dr. Talbot validates these feelings and believes that some family therapy sessions would greatly benefit Kevin and Natalie. Dr. Talbot sets up a meeting time for Natalie, Kevin, and Kevin's parents. The session will give all of them a chance to figure out how they can work together to help Kevin stay healthy.

A comprehensive treatment plan is the most effective way to treat schizophrenia. This means that the most effective treatment includes many different parts. Most patients require medication, individual psychotherapy, group psychotherapy, and family therapy in order to gain control over their illness. As you might imagine, this can be very costly. A 2005 study investigating the economic burden of schizophrenia in the United States revealed that the overall cost of schizophrenia in 2002 exceeded $60 billion.[17] More than half of this money goes to support people with schizophrenia who are unemployed because of their illness. Thus, although treatment is expensive, the biggest expense is the cost of supporting people with schizophrenia who are unable to work. Considering the high economic burden of schizophrenia, everyone benefits from making accessibility of treatment for schizophrenia a priority.

STRESS ON FAMILIES

Long before schizophrenia is diagnosed, relatives of someone with the disorder may begin to feel stressed. Prodromal, or early, signs of schizophrenia can emerge years before a diagnosis is made. Family members may begin to notice behavior changes in their relative. These behavior changes can cause a lot of anxiety, worry, or guilt for a family member of someone with schizophrenia.

Natalie has said that she feels responsible for Kevin. She grew up with Kevin, now lives with him, and cares for him a great deal. Now that she knows that Kevin may have developed the same disease that resulted in her father's suicide, Natalie feels guilty. She feels guilty because she is healthy whereas Kevin is suffering from schizophrenia. Most likely, Natalie is under a lot of stress. She loves her cousin and wants to help take care of him. In agreeing to help Kevin, Natalie is taking on a big responsibility. Even though she wants to help Kevin, she needs to take care of herself as well.

Family members of people with schizophrenia are under a great deal of stress every day. The schizophrenia patient becomes the priority. Family members worry about preventing relapse and keeping their loved one healthy. Unfortunately, many families must worry about their finances because they may have high hospital or medication expenses. Relatives of schizophrenia patients are always on guard for any change in the patient's behavior. Being overburdened with worry about a loved one, family members of schizophrenic patients can ignore their own needs and become depressed and anxious. In order to prevent caregiver "burnout," it is crucial that family members find support of their own.

Relatives of schizophrenia patients experience the negative effects of the **stigma** associated with mental illness. In our society, mental illness is sometimes interpreted as a sign of weakness. Some people still believe that schizophrenia is caused by bad parenting and is the fault of the family. Others think that the mentally ill just need to "get over it" and move on with their lives. This can be very difficult for someone who cares for a schizophrenic loved one. Mental illness is different from physical illness. When you see people who are physically disabled, you offer to help them by opening the door or carrying their groceries. You assume that their condition is not their fault. Mental disease, schizophrenia in particular, usually just becomes apparent to other people because someone is acting "weirdly." Instead of trying to help, most people keep a safe distance and want to ignore the person with schizophrenia. As a result, caregivers of schizophrenics can be alienated and made to feel guilty and alone.

In order to avoid being overwhelmed with the responsibility of caring for someone with schizophrenia, caregivers are urged to join a support group. A support group provides a forum for family members to share their feelings about having a schizophrenic relative. Additionally, caregivers are encouraged to take personal time away from their relative. Exercise, regular excursions out of the home, and even weekends away can provide a good vacation from the stress of dealing with someone with mental illness. Ironically, caring for a schizophrenic relative can increase the likelihood that the caregiver will develop symptoms of mental illness. Depression, anxiety, and drug and alcohol abuse are common to people who take care of relatives with schizophrenia.

HOMELESSNESS

Unfortunately, some of the most severely ill schizophrenia patients leave a safe place like a hospital or private home and eventually live on the streets. One-third of all homeless people are believed to be mentally ill, and a large proportion of those are schizophrenic. According to the Department of Health and Human Services, 6 percent of all schizophrenia patients are homeless at any one time. When schizophrenic patients are homeless, they rarely stay involved in any sort of treatment. As a result, homeless schizophrenia patients may experience a worsening of their symptoms. Even more problems may be caused by the stress of living on the streets. Poor hygiene, lack of sleep, and the threat of violence may hasten the descent into psychosis for many patients. Drug and alcohol use is common among schizophrenic homeless. When patients do not

Clea Simon: Author of *Mad House*

What would it be like to grow up in a household with a schizophrenic family member? What if you lived with two family members with schizophrenia? Author Clea Simon had just this experience and describes it in her book *Mad House*. Clea was only eight years old when her older sister Katherine developed schizophrenia. After she became ill, Katherine's behavior became erratic and sometimes violent. On one occasion, Clea remembers Katherine killing her hamster in a fit of rage. Later, her brother Daniel developed the disease while he was a freshman at Harvard University. Daniel dropped out of school and returned home to his family. Clea's life was never the same after both of her siblings developed schizophrenia. She recalls her childhood being filled with late-night phone calls from hospitals and visits from the police. She became accustomed to strange behaviors and volatile moods. Because she was close to her siblings, her brother in particular, Clea experienced tremendous loss when they developed schizophrenia. Her siblings became strangers to her and she felt isolated and alone.

Like many family members of schizophrenia patients, Clea often had to ignore her own needs in order to take care of her siblings. She felt powerless in a family in which mental illness was everywhere. She did not want to worry her parents, so she always acted happy, even when she was not. Her troubles were pushed aside so that she did not add more stress to the household. Still, Clea managed to make a life for herself. She attended Harvard University, graduated in 1983, and is a writer living in Cambridge, Massachusetts.

take their medications, they might try drugs or alcohol in an attempt to manage their symptoms. Unfortunately, substance use, as discussed later in this chapter, can be especially harmful to schizophrenia patients. All in all, the combination of homelessness and schizophrenia can be extremely problematic for both schizophrenia patients and society.

Schizophrenia patients become homeless for a variety of reasons. Inadequate funding can create a shortage of institutions to house those with schizophrenia. Also, schizophrenia symptoms can cause patients to leave a safe environment. Some patients hear voices that tell them to leave because someone is harming them. Others might believe that the situation they are in is causing their symptoms and leave home in hopes that a new location will make the symptoms disappear. How long they stay away varies—some patients return after only a few days, but many others return to treatment only after being brought in by the police or a social service agency. When someone with schizophrenia is missing, caregivers try to remember what, if any, places the patient may have mentioned wanting to visit. They may call the police or the hospital to help track down their relative. Unfortunately, some patients feel compelled to stay away from home and out of treatment. One solution for caregivers to help them keep track of their relative is to only give them small amounts of money. The patient will then be forced to return home in order to obtain more money, helping the relative monitor the patient's whereabouts and symptoms.

VIOLENCE AND TROUBLE WITH THE LAW

People who exhibit unpredictable behavior can be frightening. Likewise, patients with schizophrenia often behave in ways that are difficult to understand and sometimes scary. Although the media tends to link schizophrenia and violence, research has

Criminalizing the mentally ill

Thousands of mentally ill Americans in prison aren't getting the psychiatric care they need according to a report from the Human Rights Watch. The report also suggested that prison populations have a disproportionately high rate of mentally ill people.

Mentally ill more likely to be incarcerated

	State prison	Federal prison	Local jail
Mentally ill	3.9%*	3.9%	6.9%
Others	1.2%	0.3%	2.9%

Prisons have disproportionately high rate of psychoses
In a 1998 report an estimated 8 percent to 19 percent have significant psychiatric disabilities.**

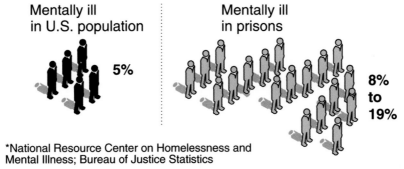

Mentally ill in U.S. population — 5%

Mentally ill in prisons — 8% to 19%

*National Resource Center on Homelessness and Mental Illness; Bureau of Justice Statistics

** "The Treatment of Offenders with Mental Disorders" edited by Robert M. Wittstein

SOURCE: "Ill-Equipped: U.S. Prisons and Offenders with Mental Illness," Human Rights Watch

AP

Figure 6.1 This graphic shows the disproportionately high rate of mentally ill people in prisons. © *AP Images*

shown that the majority of patients with schizophrenia are no more likely to be violent than someone without schizophrenia. Most schizophrenia patients prefer to be alone and rarely wish to interact with other people. When violence does occur, it is most likely to be directed at family members or treatment team members rather than strangers.

One group of schizophrenia patients that is more prone to violence includes those who abuse alcohol or illegal drugs. In fact, a recent study in the *American Journal of Psychiatry* investigated the current relationship among schizophrenia, criminal behavior, and drug abuse.[18] The study revealed that over the past 25 years, 22 percent of schizophrenia patients were convicted of a crime compared to only 8 percent of nonschizophrenics. At the same time, drug use among schizophrenia patients also increased. Whereas 25 years ago only 8 percent of schizophrenics used drugs, currently more than 26 percent have been found to use illegal drugs. Most schizophrenia patients are nonviolent, but patients who use illegal drugs may be more likely to commit a crime.

SUICIDE

On average, about one out of 10 schizophrenic patients commits suicide. The high risk of suicide in schizophrenia is due in large part to the depression and paranoia that characterize the disorder. Some patients hear voices telling them to hurt themselves. As a result, caregivers of schizophrenia patients must be on guard for signs of self-harm and possible suicide. In the general nonschizophrenic population, men are more likely than women to commit suicide, whereas women are more likely to attempt it but to be unsuccessful. This is also the case among schizophrenia patients. Men are more likely to try lethal methods of suicide such as using a gun or jumping in front of a train, whereas women are more likely to take an overdose of pills or cut themselves. Patients who are most at risk of committing suicide are in the first few years of their illness. In *Surviving Schizophrenia,* Dr. E. Fuller Torrey suggested that those patients who are at the most risk of committing suicide know that they are sick and are hopeless about the future. They may not respond well to medication and understand that their previous level of functioning is no longer attainable. These feelings may lead to frustration and depression and lead patients to believe that there is no way out of their illness. Suicide, then, becomes the perceived only option and a last resort.

Although schizophrenia patients may plan and execute a suicide attempt, many patients die accidentally by their own hand. A patient might become psychotic and enter a dangerous situation. For example, patients might believe that they can fly and jump out of a window. A recent example of an accidental suicide is the shooting of Rigoberto Alpizar. Alpizar was a passenger on an American Airlines flight leaving Miami, Florida. Before the flight took off, he allegedly demanded to get off the plane and said that he had a bomb in his backpack. Air marshals demanded that he surrender and lie on the ground but he refused, instead reaching for his backpack. As a result, Alpizar was shot and killed on the jetway. No bomb was found on his person or in his luggage. After the shooting, Alpizar's wife claimed that he was mentally ill and hadn't been taking his medication. She believed that his strange behavior was psychotic and due to his illness. Although we don't know why Alpizar behaved as he did, many suspect that this was a form of suicide caused by psychotic symptoms.

Caregivers of schizophrenia patients are encouraged to be vigilant about depressive signs, changes in behaviors, or indications that hallucinations or delusions are encouraging the patient to hurt himself. Therapists should be contacted immediately, and sometimes patients need to be hospitalized to ensure their safety. Although many people assume that talk of suicide is simply a call for attention, all suicidal behaviors must be taken seriously, especially in people with schizophrenia.

DUAL-DIAGNOSIS PATIENTS: SCHIZOPHRENIA AND SUBSTANCE ABUSE

Patients with schizophrenia who abuse drugs or alcohol are called **dual-diagnosis** patients. A dual-diagnosis patient has two diagnoses; in this case, schizophrenia and substance abuse. Research suggests that schizophrenia patients are at an increased risk of having a substance-abuse problem. In fact, someone with schizophrenia is more than four times more likely to have a substance-abuse problem than someone without schizophrenia.

Approximately 47 percent of patients with schizophrenia have a diagnosis of substance abuse. That's nearly one-half of all patients with schizophrenia. Substance use is a particularly serious problem for patients with schizophrenia because drug use by schizophrenia patients increases the chance that a patient will become violent or get into trouble with the law. Schizophrenic substance abusers are less likely to benefit from traditional treatment. They are more likely to refuse to take their medication, are less likely to respond to psychological treatments, and have poorer overall functioning and an increased chance of relapse. As a result, dual-diagnosis patients end up costing society a great deal. They require more financial resources in terms of legal intervention and repeated psychological treatment. The unique economic burden of dual-diagnosis patients has driven researchers to figure out how best to treat these complicated problems.

Why would schizophrenia patients be more likely to abuse drugs or alcohol? To begin, many schizophrenia patients use drugs because they believe that they might help relieve their symptoms. Some patients use drugs or alcohol *instead* of taking prescription medication, a process called **self-medicating**. Unfortunately, some drugs, such as cocaine or methamphetamine, can actually make schizophrenia symptoms worse. Patients who are taking their medication and still use drugs may find that the drugs interfere with the good effects of their medication.

One's living or social environment, specifically one in which there is increased access to drugs, can make it more likely that schizophrenic patients become drug abusers. **Downward drift**, a theory you read about in Chapter 4, suggests that patients with schizophrenia may live in poorer neighborhoods as a function of their mental illness. Drugs may be more accessible in impoverished neighborhoods.

Finally, the symptoms of schizophrenia, specifically poor interpersonal skills, might lead some patients to associate with people who use drugs. In an attempt to find a community, someone with schizophrenia might find it easier to be accepted by people whose lives revolve around drug use. In this situation, someone with schizophrenia might start using drugs in order to fit in. Living with schizophrenia as part of one's identity is a challenge and one that is difficult for society to accept. Perhaps some patients with schizophrenia find it easier to live as a drug addict rather than as someone with mental illness. All in all, schizophrenia patients who abuse drugs and alcohol can be problematic for treatment professionals.

Where does a schizophrenia patient with a substance abuse problem go for help? In the past 20 years, clinicians and researchers have realized the need for a treatment program for dual-diagnosis patients. Research has shown that dual-diagnosis patients need help managing both disorders in order to improve their chances of recovery. As a result, many hospitals or treatment settings now have dual-diagnosis treatment programs especially designed for these challenging patients. In a dual-diagnosis program, clinicians will focus on features of schizophrenia and substance abuse. Most important, they will address the implications of the combination of these disorders. Dual-diagnosis treatment builds upon standard medication and therapy. Some patients may need housing assistance to help them move away from an environment that allows them easy access to drugs. Other patients might need to learn behavioral skills to help them avoid or say no to drugs or alcohol. Finally, many patients need to learn money management skills from their treatment team. When access to money is limited, access to drugs is limited as well. Making sure a patient is accountable for where each dollar is spent can help the patient avoid using drugs.

Caring for someone with schizophrenia can cause family members great stress and they are encouraged to find support for themselves. Family members worry about their relatives becoming homeless or committing suicide, both common occurrences in patients with schizophrenia. Most schizophrenia patients are not particularly violent or likely to get into trouble with the law. Dual-diagnosis patients pose a unique challenge to treatment and society at large.

Outlook for the Future

7

Three months after his hospitalization, Kevin returned home to live with his parents. It has been a difficult adjustment, but he feels like he is getting better every day. Kevin was in the hospital for two months and then lived in a community home for the mentally ill for four weeks. Because his parents live within walking distance of his treatment program, Kevin plans to stay with them until he is ready to be on his own.

Dr. Talbot and the rest of Kevin's treatment team are pleased with Kevin's progress. Kevin takes his medication regularly and goes to his treatment meetings every day. He monitors what he eats, how much he sleeps, and any change in behavior or thoughts. He walks to the hospital every day and works out in the gym three times a week. As a result, Kevin is in good shape and has lost the weight he gained as a side effect of his medication. Kevin keeps a journal and reviews it with Dr. Talbot once a week. Keeping a journal helps Kevin identify warning signs of potential relapse. So far, he feels pretty good.

In order to support himself, Kevin has decided to apply for Social Security Disability Income. His case manager is helping him fill out the paperwork. Although Kevin would like to return to the radio station, he's not sure whether he is ready for the stress of a daily job. He's thinking that he will volunteer there a few hours a week to begin, and, if he continues to improve, he may return to work in a few months.

As for Natalie, she visits Kevin several times a week. She is relieved to see him doing so well and has told him that he may move back in with her if he chooses. Natalie meets with Dr. Talbot individually from time to time and also goes to family therapy sessions. Surprisingly, Kevin's illness has helped their whole family grow closer. They are all working as a team to support Kevin and one other. Kevin has a long road to recovery, but he is well on his way.

Although there are several types of treatment for schizophrenia, there still is no cure. Some patients have such severe symptoms that they do not respond to any existing treatments. Others find the side effects from medication too bothersome, so for them the costs of treatment outweigh the benefits. There remain many questions about schizophrenia that can only be answered by thoughtful research. For example, exactly how effective are existing treatment methods? How do we figure out how well a treatment program works? What can we do next to help treat the next generation of schizophrenia sufferers?

HOW DO WE DETERMINE IF A TREATMENT IS WORKING?

Measuring treatment quality is important if treatment professionals wish to improve it. If you don't know if something is broken, how will you know that it needs to be fixed? There are several ways of measuring treatment effectiveness. One way is to look at treatment outcome. If patients take their medication and their schizophrenia symptoms worsen, they do not have a good outcome. Another way to measure how a treatment is working is through **compliance**. If patients stick with their treatment and participate in it, then they are treatment compliant. If a patient is not compliant with a specific treatment it may mean one of the following: 1) the treatment itself if causing harm and the patient stops taking it in order to feel better, 2) there are other variables in the patient's life that are making it difficult to continue treatment, or 3) the treatment works so well the patient thinks they are cured and stops taking their medication. Measuring treatment compliance can help clinicians figure out what part of a specific treatment is working and what needs to be changed.

Measuring treatment success is difficult. Information about outcome might come from several sources. A therapist might record his impression of a patient at the beginning of treatment and then at the end. Alternatively, treatment success might be measured by a patient's report of his or her own progress. Some outcome measures include questionnaires or worksheets that are completed multiple times over treatment.

All these options have their strengths and weaknesses. One weakness is that outcome measures can be biased. Because therapists want to believe that they are helping their patients, they might believe they see improvement even when there is none. Alternatively, a patient might be motivated to lie about his own progress because he wants to leave treatment. Another way that patients may provide inaccurate information about their improvement may come from a desire to please the therapist. Patients may want to make their therapists feel good and like them, and, in so doing, may pretend that their symptoms are improving. Finally, although questionnaires can be helpful at measuring symptom change, they are incomplete and can obscure other important symptoms. One example of this is measuring behaviors versus emotions. Consider the relationship between suicide and depression. You might assume that the more depressed people are, the more likely they are to be suicidal. But this is not the case. Many patients, when profoundly depressed, lack the energy to commit suicide. Thus, when their depression begins to improve, they are actually *more likely* to attempt suicide than when they were

Can Schizophrenia Be Prevented?

We wear seat belts when we drive in a car, so that we are protected if we get in an accident. When we are out in the sun, we wear sunscreen to protect our skin from the harmful effects of ultraviolet light. We know not to smoke cigarettes because it increases the likelihood that we will develop lung cancer. Are there similar preventative measures we can take to prevent schizophrenia? Are there ways by which we can slow the development of this devastating illness?

Prevention of an illness can take two forms: primary and secondary prevention. The goal of primary prevention is to prevent new cases of a disorder from ever developing. One way we can do this with schizophrenia is improving prenatal and obstetric care. Pregnancy and birth complications have been linked to schizophrenia. Clinicians and researchers speculate that by improving health and nutrition in pregnant women, we may prevent the development of schizophrenia in their offspring. There is a tremendous benefit from this approach, and there are no disadvantages. By improving prenatal care, we improve the health of the mother and the baby and increase the likelihood that both will be safe and healthy. Improving prenatal care is unlikely to cause any harm to the mother or the fetus. Still, because schizophrenia is caused by a whole host of factors, there is no guarantee that a child born to a mother who was healthy during pregnancy will not develop schizophrenia.

The goal of secondary prevention is to identify those who are most at risk of developing schizophrenia and treat them early. This approach is problematic and has been the subject of great controversy. How does one identify someone at risk for schizophrenia? Can this be done with any degree of accuracy?

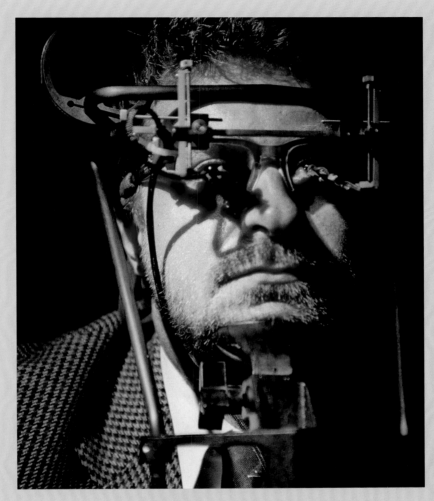

Figure 7.1 Dr. Michael Obuchowski of Hillside Hospital in Glen Oaks, N.Y. demonstrates a device that reveals how well a person's eyes track a moving laser dot. The test may help identify people who are at high risk of developing schizophrenia. © *Ed Betz/AP*

Relatives of schizophrenia patient are at risk, but not all relatives will develop the disorder. Another way researchers identify at-risk individuals is with a questionnaire that measures risk

(continues)

(continued)

for psychosis. The questionnaire measures thoughts and behaviors that have been found to be indicators of future psychotic symptoms. Research has shown that 20 percent to 45 percent of people who score highly on this scale will eventually develop full-blown psychosis. The biggest problem with the secondary prevention approach is that it yields too many false positives. In this case, a false positive is saying that people will develop schizophrenia when they will not.

So far, researchers who take the secondary prevention approach have suggested prescribing low doses of antipsychotic medications to those who are most at risk for developing the illness. That means that they give medication to people who have not developed actual symptoms. As you might imagine, this can be problematic and complicated. Some argue that it is unethical to give medication to people who are not sick. Antipsychotic medications are not without side effects and may cause long-term health problems. In addition, it may be stigmatizing to be diagnosed and/or treated for a mental illness. A person who is told he or she is at risk for schizophrenia might actually become anxious or depressed.

Current research is exploring the costs and benefits of early treatment for schizophrenia. So far, the results are inconclusive. The social and economic benefits of schizophrenia prevention are enormous. It is likely that this research will continue well into the future.

more severely depressed. If researchers are interested in how well a treatment program is working on suicide attempts, they must obtain information about both depression and suicidal thoughts and behaviors. A questionnaire might not reveal a complete picture of the patient.

Successfully measuring treatment outcome requires as comprehensive an approach as does treatment design. Researchers need to better understand the therapist-patient relationship in schizophrenia. They need to figure out how to keep a patient in treatment in order to determine whether a specific approach is working. Finally, they need to consider measuring improvement in all areas of the illness, including positive and negative symptoms, side effects, social and occupational functioning, and interpersonal skills.

Schizophrenia research progresses every day. Clinical trials examining the effectiveness of existing medications are yielding more and more information about the kinds of patients that may be helped by specific treatments. Researchers are working on developing more sophisticated medications that improve symptoms with fewer side effects. Therapists are working on designing psychological interventions that provide information and support to patients suffering from schizophrenia. Finally, social workers are focusing on how to identify the needs of patients in order to help them obtain the resources they need to live independently.

ELIMINATING MYTHS AND STIGMA OF SCHIZOPHRENIA
Unfortunately, many people know very little about schizophrenia and other forms of mental illness. Society has several misconceptions about psychiatric disorders in general, and schizophrenia in particular. The media often perpetuate myths about mental illness. When covering a story about a crime, reporters sometimes stress a history of mental illness in the alleged perpetrator even though schizophrenia patients are no more likely than people without schizophrenia to commit violent crimes. Some movies and TV programs misrepresent people with mental illness and make them appear weak, silly,

or frightening. As a result, those at risk may be less likely to seek help for mental illness. The only way to eliminate the stigma of mental illness is through education. Everyone needs to learn more about different kinds of mental disease and their causes, effects, and treatments. With better understanding of mental illness, we can hope that these harmful and inaccurate stereotypes are eradicated.

NARSAD, the National Alliance for Research on Schizophrenia and Depression, is a nonprofit agency devoted to providing funding for research that helps us learn more about mental illness. In 2001, NARSAD surveyed mental health professionals in the United States and assembled a list of the most common myths about mental illness. Here are the top 10 myths about mental illness as listed by NARSAD. Following each myth is a fact that explains why the myth is a misperception.[19]

TOP TEN MYTHS ABOUT MENTAL ILLNESS

Myth #1: *Psychiatric disorders are not true medical illnesses like heart disease and diabetes. People who have a mental illness are just "crazy."*

Fact: Brain disorders, like heart disease and diabetes, are legitimate medical illnesses. Research shows there are genetic and biological causes for psychiatric disorders, and they can be treated effectively.

Myth #2: *People with a severe mental illness, such as schizophrenia, are usually dangerous and violent.*

Fact: Statistics show that the incidence of violence in people who have a brain disorder is not much higher than it is in the general population. Those suffering from a psychosis such as schizophrenia are more often frightened, confused, and despairing than violent.

Myth #3: *Mental illness is the result of bad parenting.*
　　Fact: Most experts agree that a genetic susceptibility, combined with other risk factors, leads to a psychiatric disorder. In other words, mental illnesses have a physical cause.

Myth #4: *Depression results from a personality weakness or character flaw, and people who are depressed could just snap out of it if they tried hard enough.*
　　Fact: Depression has nothing to do with being lazy or weak. It results from changes in brain chemistry or brain function, and medication and/or psychotherapy often help people recover.

Myth #5: *Schizophrenia means split personality, and there is no way to control it.*
　　Fact: Schizophrenia is often confused with multiple personality disorder. Actually, schizophrenia is a brain disorder that robs people of their ability to think clearly and logically. The estimated 2.5 million Americans with schizophrenia have symptoms ranging from social withdrawal to hallucinations and delusions. Medication has helped many of these individuals to lead fulfilling, productive lives.

Myth #6: *Depression is a normal part of the aging process.*
　　Fact: It is not normal for older adults to be depressed. Signs of depression in older people include a loss of interest in activities, sleep disturbances, and lethargy. Depression in the elderly is often undiagnosed, and it is important for seniors and their family members to recognize the problem and seek professional help.

Myth #7: *Depression and other illnesses, such as anxiety disorders, do not affect children or adolescents. Any problems they have are just a part of growing up.*

Fact: Children and adolescents can develop severe mental illnesses. In the United States, one in 10 children and adolescents has a mental disorder severe enough to cause impairment. Only about 20 percent of these children receive needed treatment. Left untreated, these problems can get worse. Anyone talking about suicide should be taken very seriously.

Myth #8: *If you have a mental illness, you can will it away. Being treated for a psychiatric disorder means an individual has in some way "failed" or is weak.*
Fact: A serious mental illness cannot be willed away. Ignoring the problem does not make it go away either. It takes courage to seek professional help.

Myth #9: *Addiction is a lifestyle choice and shows a lack of will-power. People with a substance abuse problem are morally weak or "bad."*
Fact: Addiction is a disease that generally results from changes in brain chemistry. It has nothing to do with being a "bad" person.

Myth #10: *Electroconvulsive therapy (ECT), formerly known as shock treatment, is painful and barbaric.*
Fact: ECT has given a new lease on life to many people who suffer from severe and debilitating depression. It is used when other treatments such as psychotherapy or medication fail or cannot be used. Patients who receive ECT are asleep and under anesthesia, so they do not feel anything.
(Reprinted from http://www.narsad.org.)

HOW CAN YOU HELP?
By reading this book and educating yourself about schizophrenia, you have taken the first step to help eliminate misperceptions

about this devastating illness. Now you can help stop perpetuating the cycle of misinformation that surrounds schizophrenia. When you see someone with mental illness being made fun of in the media, don't laugh. Tell whoever you're with that the joke is inappropriate and unkind. Try not to use adjectives as nouns. To call someone a "schizophrenic" implies that they are defined more by their disease than by their personality. When you see someone who appears to be mentally ill, don't be afraid—most likely he or she wants to be left alone and has no intention to harm others. Volunteer for a mental health research agency like NARSAD or NAMI, the National Alliance for the Mentally Ill. In so doing you might come into contact with family members, friends, or people with mental illness who can increase your understanding about these disorders. Finally, talk to others about mental illness. Share the knowledge you have and continue to learn more. The key to eradicating stigma is through increasing understanding.

FUTURE DIRECTIONS

Each year, more young people are diagnosed with schizophrenia. These individuals lose touch with their own reality and live in a confusing and often scary world. Physical diseases such as cancer or AIDS receive a great deal of financial support because they cause great sadness for many patients and their families. Although schizophrenia is not in itself a deadly disease, it causes equal pain. Because someone with schizophrenia is often so removed from reality, many families feel as though they have lost a loved one. To this end, researchers must continue studying what causes this mental illness and how to treat it. The government and private philanthropic organizations are needed to continue to fund research that will help us to learn more about schizophrenia. Until we can completely prevent or cure schizophrenia, there remains work to be done.

NOTES

1. American Experience, "People and Events: Recovery from Schizophrenia." Available online. URL: http://www. pbs.org/wgbh/amex/nash/ peopleevents/e_recovery.html. Accessed February 22, 2007.

2. John F. Nash Jr., "Autobiography." Availalable online. URL: http:// nobelprize.org/economics/ laureates/1994/nash-autobio.html. Accessed May 10, 2007.

3. Sylvia Nasar, *A Beautiful Mind*. New York: Simon and Schuster, 1998, 335.

4. American Experience, "Transcript." Available online. URL: http://www. pbs.org/wgbh/amex/nash/filmmore/ pt.html. Accessed February 22, 2007.

5. See note 1.

6. National Alliance on Mental Illness, "About Mental Illness." Available online. URL: http://www.nami.org/ template.cfm?section=By_Illness. Accessed February 22, 2007.

7. Robert L. Spitzer et al., eds., *DSM-IV-TR Casebook: A Learning Companion to the Diagnostic and Statistical Manual of Mental Disorders*. 4th ed., Text Revision. (Washington, DC: American Psychiatric Publishing, 2004), 189–90.

8. H. Häfner et al., "The Influence of Age and Sex on the Onset and Early Course of Schizophrenia." *British Journal of Psychiatry* 162 (1993): 80–86.

9. E. Fuller Torrey, *Surviving Schizophrenia: A Manual for Families, Consumers and Providers, 3rd ed.* New York: Harper Perennial, 1995, p. 79.

10. G.A. Fava and R. Kellner, "Prodromal Symptoms in Affective Disorders." *American Journal of Psychiatry* 148 (1991): 828–830.

11. British Columbia Schizophrenia Society, "Basic Facts about Schizophrenia," Available online. URL: http://www.mentalhealth.com/book/ p40-sc02.html#Head_4. Downloaded on November 13, 2006.

12. Quoted in J.N. Butcher, S. Mineka, and J.M. Hooley, *Abnormal Psychology*. Pearson: Boston, 2004.

13. Harrison et al., "Recovery from Psychotic Illness: A 15- and 25-year International Follow-up Study." *British Journal of Psychiatry* 178 (2001): 506–517.

14. N.C. Andreasen, "The Role of the Thalamus in Schizophrenia." *Canadian Journal of Psychiatry* 42 (1997): 27–33.

15. J. Hooley and S. Candela, "Interpersonal Functioning in Schizophrenia." In *Oxford Textbook of Psychopathology*, edited by T. Million, P.H. Blaney, and R.D. Davis. New York: Oxford University Press, 1999.

16. J.D. Hegarty et al., "One Hundred Years of Schizophrenia: A Meta Analysis of the Outcome Literature." *American Journal of Psychiatry* 151, no. 10 (1994): 1409–1416.

17. E.Q. Wu et al., "The Economic Burden of Schizophrenia in the United States in 2002." *Journal of Clinical Psychiatry* 66, no. 9 (2005): 1122–1129.

18. C. Wallace, P.E. Mullen, and P. Burgess, "Criminal Offending in Schizophrenia over a 25-year Period Marked by Deinstitutionalization and Increasing Prevalence of Comorbid Substance Use Disorders." *American Journal of Psychiatry*, 161 (2004): 716–727.

19. Suicide and Mental Health Association International, "NARSAD Publishes Top 10 Myths About Mental Illness Based on Nationwide Survey." Available online. URL: http://suicideandmentalhealth associationinternational.org/ factsmythsment.html. Accessed February 22, 2007.

GLOSSARY

active stage—Period of schizophrenia where intense symptoms are present.

adoption studies—Studies of biological and adoptive relatives of persons with and without schizophrenia to determine genetic versus environmental influences.

affect—Emotion.

agranulocytosis—Serious condition occasionally resulting from certain antipsychotic medications that involves a sudden drop in white blood cell count.

alogia—Inability to speak. A symptom of schizophrenia.

ambivalence—Mixed feelings or emotions.

anhedonia—Inability to feel pleasure or enjoyment.

associations—A connection between thoughts or feelings.

atypical antipsychotic medications—A newer type of schizophrenia medications that treat both positive and negative symptoms with fewer side effects.

autism—Difficulty living in reality; confusion between fantasy and real life.

autonomic arousal—Physical signs of emotion. Examples include a fast heartbeat and sweaty palms.

avolition—Lack of motivation.

bipolar disorder—Mood disorder in which a person experiences depression and feelings of extreme happiness or energy.

blunted affect—Inability to show appropriate emotion, even to extreme events.

case manager—Someone who helps schizophrenia patients secure housing, financial support, or a job. A case manager helps schizophrenia patients with their basic, daily needs.

catatonic schizophrenia—A type of schizophrenia characterized by movement problems. Some patients with schizophrenia, catatonic type, might hold rigid postures for a long period of time.

cerebrospinal spinal fluid—A clear fluid that is found in the space between the skull and the brain, and in the spinal column.

clang associations—A symptom of schizophrenia in which a person uses rhymes that make little sense.

chlorpromazine—One of the earliest medications for schizophrenia.

communication deviance—Unclear speech that is difficult to understand. Communication deviance appears to contribute to relapse in schizophrenia.

compliance—Ability to remain in treatment.

concordant—Sharing a trait. When both members of a twin pair have schizophrenia, they are concordant for the disorder.

cortisol—A stress hormone.

delusion of grandeur—False belief that one is a famous or important person.

delusion of guilt—False belief that one is to blame for some terrible event.

delusion of reference—False belief that environmental events convey special meaning to a person.

delusions—Bizarre beliefs that are held with absolute conviction.

disorganized speech—Speech that is difficult to understand and may be nonsensical.

disorganized symptoms—Symptoms of schizophrenia in which a patient exhibits thoughts and behavior that are confused and disorganized.

dopamine—A neurotransmitter that is involved in schizophrenia.

downward drift—A sociological theory that suggests that schizophrenia patients are more likely to be poor because their illness ensures that they will drift downward into the lower socioeconomic levels.

dual-diagnosis—Having two diagnoses; in this case, of schizophrenia and a substance-use disorder.

echolalia—Repetition of words, like a parrot.

echopraxia—Repetition of behavior, mimicking actions.

electroconvulsive therapy (ECT)—Use of electricity to produce seizures and unconsciousness. ECT has been used to treat schizophrenia. ECT is helpful for severe mood disorders and some psychotic symptoms.

emotional overinvolvement—A type of expressed emotion in which a family member is excessively involved with the patient.

erotomania—False belief that one is romantically involved with someone else.

expressed emotion—A type of negative communication in which family members direct hostile, critical, or overly emotional comments to a patient with mental illness.

extra-pyramidal side effects (EPS)—Side effects from antipsychotic medication in which patients tremble or shake.

false positives—Identifying the presence of illness when it is not there.

fever therapy—An out-of-date method of treating schizophrenia in which high fevers are induced.

genetic—Having to do with genes or heredity. Running in families.

glutamate—A neurotransmitter that is involved in schizophrenia.

gustatory hallucinations—An experience in which someone tastes something that isn't really there.

hallucinations—False perceptions or experiences of things that are not real.

haloperidol—A medication used to treat schizophrenia.

hebephrenia—Another word for disorganized schizophrenia.

lobotomy—Brain surgery in which connections to the frontal lobes are severed.

major depression—A severe mood disorder in which someone experiences depressed mood and other symptoms for at least two weeks.

metabolite—A substance that is produced during the breakdown of a neurotransmitter and can be used to measure how much neurotransmitter is being used.

misdiagnoses—Errors in diagnosis.

negative symptom—Symptoms that reflect an absence of a behavior that should be there.

negativistic—Aggressive behaviors in which someone refuses to cooperate or does the complete opposite of what he is asked.

neuroleptics—Antipsychotic medications.

neurons—Cells in the brain.

neurotransmitters—Chemical messengers in the brain. See dopamine, glutamate.

obsessive compulsive disorder—A mental disorder characterized by unwanted thoughts or images and/or repetitive behaviors.

olfactory hallucinations—An experience in which someone smells something that isn't really there.

outcome—Effectiveness of treatment.

persecutory delusion—A false belief in which someone is convinced that others are planning to hurt them.

perseveration—Repeating the same thought or behavior unnecessarily.

personal therapy—Type of individual psychotherapy in which patients work one-on-one with a therapist to learn coping and life skills.

positive symptom—Symptom of schizophrenia in which a behavior is present that should not be there.

probands—In a heredity study, the person who has the disorder (i.e., the schizophrenia patient).

prodromal stage—The first, early stage of schizophrenia in which symptoms begin to appear.

psychoanalysis—An intense form of individual therapy created by Sigmund Freud.

psychotic—Behaviors that demonstrate that an individual has lost contact with reality.

relapse—Return of active stage of schizophrenia after a short period when symptoms lessened.

remission—Period of significant improvement that may be brief or permanent.

residual stage—Period of time immediately following the acute stage of schizophrenia in which most, but not all, symptoms have disappeared.

reuptake—Process in which one neuron reabsorbs the excess neurotransmitter after it has performed its function.

risk factors—Qualities that increase the odds that someone will develop a disorder such as schizophrenia.

schizoaffective disorder—A disorder in which psychotic and mood disorder symptoms are present.

self-medicating—Using nonprescription drugs or alcohol to treat symptoms of a mental disorder.

social drift hypothesis—A sociological theory that suggests that the people with schizophrenia drift downward on the socioecomonic ladder because their symptoms limit them socially and occupationally.

sociogenic hypothesis—A sociological theory that suggests that the stress caused by living at a lower socioeconomic level increases the likelihood that one will develop a mental disorder.

somatic delusion—A false belief that something is happening to one's body.

stigma—In psychological terms, the negative associations that accompany being part of a group or having a psychiatric diagnosis.

subtype diagnosis—A specific diagnosis given to schizophrenia patients that describes the type, or prominent symptoms, in the presentation.

symptom profile—The set of symptoms that any one patient experiences.

synapse—The space between two neurons through which neurotransmitters are shared and information is passed.

tactile hallucinations—False sensory experiences in which someone feels something physically that is not there.

tardive dyskinesia—Neurological condition that results from the use of antipsychotic medications.

thalamus—The area of the brain that translates and transfers sensory information.

thought control—A symptom of schizophrenia in which patients believe that their thoughts are being controlled by someone or something.

twin studies—Studies of concordance rates in twin pairs that allow researchers to consider the effect of genes and environment on the development of a disorder.

typical antipsychotic medications—Early medications for schizophrenia that affect global dopamine function.

ventricles—Fluid-filled spaces in the center of the brain.

warning sign—A behavior or sign that indicates that a patient might be likely to relapse.

Wisconsin Card Sort Test (WCST)—A neuropsychological task that tests one's concentration and attention.

word salad—Extremely bizarre and nonsensical words used by patients with schizophrenia.

FURTHER RESOURCES

Books and Articles

American Psychiatric Association. *Diagnostic and Statistical Manual of Mental Disorders*, 4th ed. Washington, DC: American Psychiatric Association, 2000.

Beck, A.T., and A. Freeman and associates. *Cognitive Therapy of Personality Disorders*. New York: Guilford, 1990.

Butcher, J.N., S. Mineka, and J.M. Hooley. *Abnormal Psychology*. Boston: Pearson, 2004.

Butzlaff, R.L. and J.M. Hooley. "Expressed emotion and psychiatric relapse: A meta-analysis." *Archives of General Psychiatry*, 55, no. 6 (1998): 647–652.

Green, M.F. *Schizophrenia Revealed: From Neurons to Social Interactions*. New York: Norton, 2001.

Hooley, J.M., and M.L. Delgado. "Pain insensitivity in relatives of patients with schizophrenia and bipolar disorder." In *Principles of Experimental Psychopathology: Essays in Honor of Brendan Maher*, edited by M.F. Lenzenweger and J.M. Hooley, 157–171. Washington, DC: American Psychological Association, 2001.

Johnson, Angela. *Humming Whispers*. New York: Franklin Watts, 2005.

Kopelowicz, A., R.P. Liberman, and R. Zarate. "Psychosocial treatments for schizophrenia." In *A Guide to Treatments that Work, 2nd ed.*, edited by P.E. Nathan and J.M. Gorman, 201–228. New York: Oxford University Press, 2001.

Kring, A.M., and J.M. Neale. "Do schizophrenic patients show a disjunctive relationship among expressive, experiential, and psychophysiological components of emotion?" *Journal of Abnormal Psychology*, 105 (1996): 249–257.

Landau, Elaine. *Schizophrenia*. New York: Franklin Watts, 2005.

Mednick, S.A., R.A. Machon, M.O. Huttunen, and D. Bonnet. "Adult schizophrenia following prenatal exposure to an influenza epidemic." *Archives of General Psychiatry*, 45 (1988): 189–192.

Torrey, E. Fuller, et al. *Schizophrenia and Manic-Depressive Disorder: The Biological Roots of Mental Illness as Revealed by the Landmark Study of Identical Twins.* New York: Basic Books, 1994.

Rosenthal, D. *The Genain Quadruplets.* New York: Basic Books, 1963.

Wahlberg, K.E., L.C. Wynne, et al. "Gene-environment interaction in vulnerability to schizophrenia: Findings from the Finnish adoptive family study of schizophrenia." *American Journal of Psychiatry*, 154, no. 3 (1997): 355–362.

Walker, Elaine F., K.E. Grimes, D.M. Davis, and A.J. Smith. "Childhood precursors of schizophrenia: Facial expressions of emotion." *American Journal of Psychiatry,* 150, no. 11 (1993): 1654–1660.

Weinberger, D.R. "Implications of normal brain development for the pathogenesis of schizophrenia." *Archives of General Psychiatry*, 44 (1987): 660–669.

Web Sites

The DANA Foundation: Brainy Kids

http://www.dana.org/kids/

Laboratory for Adolescent Science

http://theteenbrain.org

The National Alliance on Mental Illness

http://www.nami.org

National Alliance for Research on Schizophrenia and Depression

http://www.narsad.org

The National Institute of Mental Health: Schizophrenia

http://www.nimh.nih.gov/healthinformation/schizophreniamenu.cfm

Schizophrenia.com (Nonprofit Source of Information about Schizophrenia)

http://www.schizophrenia.com

Schizophrenia: A Handbook for Families

http://www.mentalhealth.com/book/p40-sc01.html#Head_4

INDEX

economic burden of schizophrenia, in United States, 76

ECT. *See* electroconvulsive therapy

EE. *See* expressed emotion

electroconvulsive therapy (ECT), 6, 61, 96, 101

"Emilio" (schizophrenic patient), 13–14
  clang speech, 20
  disorganized symptoms, 15
  undifferentiated schizophrenia, 25

emotion. *See* affect

emotional experience, 22–23

emotional overinvolvement, 58, 101

environmental causes
  and adoption studies, 43–46
  and brain architecture, vi–vii
  and lack of relatives with disease, 12
  and twin studies, 43

EPS. *See* extra-pyramidal side effects

erotomania, 30, 102

experience, and brain architecture, viii–ix

experience-dependent development, viii

expressed emotion (EE), 57–58, 70–71, 102

extra-pyramidal side effects (EPS), 63, 102

eye contact, 69

facial expressiveness, 23

false positives, 92, 102

family environment, as cause of schizophrenia, 44–46, 57–58

family members
  identification of warning signs by, 33–35
  impact of schizophrenia on, 76–80

family studies, 42–43

family therapy, 70–71, 88

famine, 49

fever therapy, 61, 102

first-person accounts of schizophrenia, 26–28

flu. *See* influenza, prenatal exposure to

folie à deux, 30

Foster, Jodie, 64–65

Fox, Valerie, 26–28

fraternal twins, 43

Freud, Sigmund, 67, 68

frontal lobes, 50

future outlook, 87–97
  determining effectiveness of treatment, 88–89, 92–93
  eliminating myths and stigma, 93–97
  prevention, 90–92

gender, as factor, 14, 38–39

genes, brain architecture and, vi–viii

genetics, 12, 44–46, 102

Genian Quadruplets, 44–45

glutamate, 54, 56, 102

Green, Michael, 70

gustatory hallucinations, 19, 102

hallucinations
  auditory (*See* auditory hallucinations)
  and CBT, 69
  defined, 102
  and paranoid schizophrenia, 24
  as part of diagnostic criteria, 19
  as positive symptom, 2, 15

hallucinogenic drugs, 56

haloperidol, 61, 102

hebephrenia, 24, 102

Hecker, Ewald, 24

Hegarty, J. D., 73

Hinckley, John, Jr., 64–66

history, of schizophrenia, 2–11

homelessness, 28, 78, 80

Hooley, Jill, 37, 58

hostility, by family members, 58

HVA, 55

identical twins, 43

illegal drugs, 54. *See also* substance abuse

influenza, prenatal exposure to, 47, 48

insensitivity to pain, 36–37

institutionalization, 4–6, 28, 61

insulin coma therapy, 6, 9

interpersonal skills. *See* social skills training

and prevention, 92

and relatives of patients, 77–78

stimulants, dopamine function and, 54

straitjacket, 61, 62

stress

and brain architecture, viii

and cortisol, 58

in families, 76–78

management of, 72–73

of psychoanalysis, 67

substance abuse, 84–86

among caregivers, 78

dangers of, 72

and drug-induced psychosis, 30

and homelessness, 78, 80

and violence, 82

subtype diagnosis, 24–25

suicide, 82–83

and depression, 89, 92

prevalence of, 35–36, 82–83

support groups

for caregivers, 78

for families, 70

Surviving Schizophrenia (E. Fuller Torrey), 14–15, 82–83

symptom(s), 22–23

symptom categories, 14–18

symptom profile, 18, 104

synapse, vi, ix, 53, 54, 104

tactile hallucinations, 19, 104

"Talbot, Dr." (clinician), 60–61, 75–76, 87, 88

tardive dyskinesia, 63, 104

Taxi Driver (movie), 64

thalamus, 51–52, 104

therapy. *See* psychological treatments

Thorazine (chlorpromazine). *See* chlorpromazine

thought control, 19, 104

Torrey, E. Fuller, 14–15, 82–83

treatment, 60–73

atypical antipsychotic medication, 63, 66

case management, 71

cognitive behavioral therapy, 67–69

determining effectiveness of, 88–89, 92–93

for dual-diagnosis patients, 85–86

early history of, 4–7, 61, 62

family therapy, 70–71

homelessness and, 78

medication (*See* antipsychotic medication)

outcome, 73–74

psychological, 66–71

psychotherapy, 67

relapse prevention, 71–73

social skills training, 69–70

typical antipsychotic medication, 61–63

twin studies, 43, 104

typical antipsychotic medication, 61–63, 104

undifferentiated schizophrenia, 25

ventricles, 48–49, 104

vesicle, 53

violence, 80–82

homelessness and, 78

myths about, 94

voices, hearing. *See* auditory hallucinations

Wahlberg, Karl-Erik, 46

Walker, Elaine, 33

warning signs

defined, 105

of onset, 34–35

of relapse, 71–72

WCST. *See* Wisconsin Card Sort Test

Weinberger, Daniel, 56

willpower, myths about, 96

winter, birth during, 47

Wisconsin Card Sort Test (WCST), 50–51, 105

women, 38, 82. *See also* gender, as factor

word salad, 20, 105

Zoloft, 54

Heather Barnett Veague attended the University of California, Los Angeles, and received her Ph.D. in psychology from Harvard University in 2004. She is the author of several journal articles investigating information processing and the self in borderline personality disorder. Currently, she is the Director of Clinical Research for the Laboratory of Adolescent Sciences at Vassar College. Dr. Veague lives in Stockbridge, Massachusetts, with her husband and children.

Islamophobia

Deal with it

in the name of peace

Safia Saleh
Illustrated by Hana Shafi

James Lorimer & Company Ltd., Publishers
Toronto

You're excited to see everyone at school after a long summer. You're even more eager to show off your new look — the head scarf you've decided to start wearing. On the first day of school, you run over to greet your friends. You're surprised at their reaction. You get some hesitant "Hellos," and no one seems to know what to say to you. None of them say anything about your hijab.

What's going on?

The day passes and it gets even weirder. You get awkward stares from other students and even teachers. At lunch, a friend asks you quietly if everything is all right at home. She says she is sorry you now have to wear a hijab.

Is this what Islamophobia feels like?

Islamophobia is a kind of intolerance, or a refusal to accept and respect ideas and views that are different from your own. It is the belief that Muslims, or people who follow the religion of Islam, are a group to be fearful of. It can lead to intolerant, and even hateful, speech and actions. If you have seen or been a part of conflict based on Islamophobia, this book can help you protect yourself, recognize your own biases, and stand up for someone being treated unfairly.

Contents

What is Islamophobia?

Treating people unfairly because of their faith is discrimination, and it is wrong. Some examples of Islamophobia are pretty obvious when we see them:

- Being afraid that Muslim people are going to hurt you.
- Hurting someone because they are Muslim.
- Telling a Muslim to "go back where you came from."
- Making fun of a Muslim person's clothing.
- Not inviting a Muslim kid to a party because they are Muslim.

But what about:

- Thinking all Muslims are terrorists?
- Believing that Muslim women and girls have no rights?
- Believing Muslims want to take over your country?
- Asking a Muslim if they are allowed to go to school?
- Questioning or teasing a Muslim girl for wearing a hijab?
- Teasing a fasting Muslim with food?

Whether these things happen because someone doesn't understand what Islam is, or because someone is targeting Muslims, Islamophobic attitudes can lead to conflict.

Islam is a religion. People who practise Islam follow the will of Allah, the One God. The word Islam comes from the Arabic word *salaam*, which means "peace."

A **Muslim** is a person who follows the religion of Islam.

Muslims follow the message of the **Qur'an**, the Holy Book, revealed to the prophet Muhammad by Allah.

5

Islamophobia can be

based on...

Islamophobia 101

QUIZ

When someone is targeted for being Muslim, that is Islamophobia. But sometimes what people do or say has to do with the person, not the fact that they are Muslim. Read the following scenarios and decide if they are examples of Islamophobia or not.

1 In the Extreme

When the class is talking about current events, Jimmy asks Abdul if he knows extremist Muslims.

Not Islamophobia: Not all Muslims are extreme. Most Muslims don't like extremist thinking and actions, just like everyone else.

2 Unkindest Cut

Soyab is not very athletic and is always picked last to play on the basketball team during recess.

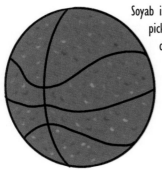

Not Islamophobia: If Soyab is always picked last because he isn't good at basketball, it has nothing to do with his being Muslim

3 Blow Up

Muhammad is tossed a note in class. When he unfolds the paper, all that is written on it is "Boom!"

Islamophobia: The reference is to the idea that all Muslims are terrorist threats. Muhammad is being targeted for being Muslim.

4 Airport Anxiety

When Syed's family travels, they always get "randomly selected" at the airport for extra screening. They are brought to a separate room where they are asked questions and their baggage is opened and gone through.

Islamophobia: Syed's family look Muslim and people assume they are Muslim, so they get screened more often.

5 Pizza Your Mind

The team has ordered pizza after the game, but Daniyal is upset because there is no vegetarian pizza for him. He is told to just pick the ham off his slice.

Maybe: This might be based on the team not knowing or understanding what halal food (meat that is blessed and acknowledged and provides a different option when pork is served) is, or they might have just forgotten. In any case, it is inconsiderate to not respect people's needs.

6 Bus Stop Bluster

Adam is waiting for a bus when he overhears a man complaining that refugees are taking over their city.

Maybe: Refugees in general could mean anyone of any faith, but this behaviour is intolerant because it is based on the assumption that all refugees are a threat to the economy and to public safety.

7 Giving Granny Grief

A group of kids on the playground see Ibrahim's grandmother bring him a book he forgot. They tease her and call her a Ninja Lady because she wears a burka, which is a veil that covers her face.

Not necessarily Islamophobia: But it could be intolerance, since what Ibrahim's grandmother wears is being judged because it is different.

8 Playing the Villain

On Halloween William dresses up as a Middle Eastern guy with a pretend sword. He really plays it up, making threatening motions and speaking in what he thinks is an Arab accent.

Islamophobia: Dressing up as an Arab with a sword supports the idea that Muslims are violent. Making anyone's cultural background a costume spreads stereotypes and shows disrespect for that culture.

9 To Her Face

Ayesha's friend tells her she looks prettier when she doesn't wear a hijab.

Islamophobia: By treating Ayesha's decision to wear a hijab as fashion, her friend is not respecting Ayesha's beliefs.

10 BFFs

Fatima is the new girl in school, and she has just arrived from Pakistan. Akasha wants to welcome her, but her best friend Kim tells her not to speak to Fatima.

Maybe: It depends on Kim's reasons for not wanting Akasha to be friendly with Fatima. It could be jealousy, possessiveness, racism, or Islamophobia — or a combination of all these things.

Islamophobia 101

Dear Conflict Counsellor

Q: **The Muslim kids in my school get together at lunchtime on Friday to pray. Sometimes they arrive late to class by ten minutes after praying and never get in trouble. Why do they get special permission to do something they should be doing at home? It doesn't seem fair to me.**

— *Not a Prayer*

A: Fairness is about giving everyone the same thing, even if they don't need or want it. Equity is giving people what they need so they can feel positive about themselves. Your Muslim classmates need to pray at a specific time as part of their faith and as part of their identity. When your teacher gives a little extra time to your Muslim classmates to return after prayer, it is because schools have to make accommodations for kids based on a religious need.

Q: **I'm confused because I heard that Muslims aren't allowed to enter some countries, including the United States. I live in Canada, but the best part of my summer holidays is the time I spend with my American cousins. I'm worried that I won't be allowed to visit them, and if they leave the US, they won't be allowed back home.**

— *Border-Crosser*

A: Laws that don't allow some people from some countries to come into the United States continue to be an issue. Those countries are considered Muslim countries, but that doesn't mean that all Muslims are banned. Everyday, Muslims peacefully cross international borders, including those between the US and Canada. If you speak to your family about your concerns, they will make sure everything is okay for travel and visits.

Q: I'm feeling very confused. My Muslim friend showed me a video about another Muslim boy who was arrested in a school for making a clock. The boy's principal called the police because he thought it was something dangerous. This doesn't feel right. Why did they do that?

— #Just_a_clock

A: The principal assumed that the boy was making something dangerous, like a bomb, because of the stereotype of a Muslim terrorist. Making stereotypes about a whole group of people can lead to hurt and harm. Sometimes the news and movies make people think that Muslims are violent when it's not true. It is important to remember that we can't judge an entire group of people based on what we see in the movies.

Q: Some of the kids in my class talk about my Muslim friend behind his back, but they talk to him in class. I enjoy hanging out with him but I don't know if I should keep being his friend.

— Have to Choose

A: You will need to think about what makes a good friend. If a person makes fun of someone else because of their faith, are they the kind of person you want to be friends with? When other kids make fun of your Muslim friend, that is Islamophobic. It hurts people, and by letting them do it, you are hurting your friend too.

Q: My hockey team just met our new coach. He is a Muslim. We heard he has never lost a game but I'm not okay being coached by a Muslim. I think that the whole team will be treated unfairly because people don't like our coach. Why can't we have a normal coach?

— Wanna Win

A: Your coach doesn't sound normal; he sounds excellent! It takes time to get to know people enough to work with them. Not liking your coach because he is Muslim is not a good start. Why don't you take some time to talk to him, ask him questions, and get to know him better before you make a judgement? If you and your team stand up for your coach when others are Islamophobic, you can make sure that your sport stays fair.

Myths

Muslim women and girls aren't allowed to be free.

There is nothing in the Qur'an that says that women should not be allowed to get an education, vote, start a business, keep the money they earn, and many other independent actions.

Muslims are all Arabs / Middle Eastern.

Arab Muslims only represent about 15 per cent of Muslims in the world. Muslims come from all over the world. The largest Muslim majority country is Indonesia.

All people from the Middle East are Muslim.

Since this part of the world is where Christianity, Judaism, and Islam all started, there are people of all beliefs.

Muslims are racist.

Muslims believe that all people were created equally in the eyes of God.

THE HOLY QUR'AN

Muslims are violent.

Muslims believe that peace and mercy are better than any argument, conflict, or violence.

- Islam is the fastest growing religion in the world.
- Muslims believe in the same prophets as Christians and Jews.

13

The **Believer**

Every time something bad happens on the news you hold your breath, waiting and hoping that someone with a Muslim name is not to blame.

It sickens you when you know that one bad actor gives all people like you a bad name.

You are proud of your family and your faith, but it gets really hard to convince people that you can be a Muslim and still be a good person.

DEAR DR. SHRINK-WRAPPED...

Q: I love to run. At our last track and field meet, I was disqualified from my event because I was wearing hijab. No one told me about this rule until the race was over. I don't think this is fair. What can I do?

— *Runner at Heart*

A: The rule is unfair, Runner, and it's even more unfair that you were not told about it before the race. Dr. Shrink-Wrapped knows you have to be courageous to speak out against unfairness. But by reaching out to the race organizers and rule makers you can try to get the rule looked at and changed.

Q: My class is going on an overnight trip to a camp next month. As a Muslim, I am going to need special meals that are halal. I feel embarrassed having to ask for this because no one really knows I am Muslim.

— *Muslim in Hiding*

A: It is our differences that make us special, Hiding. Professional kitchens are used to special needs, such as allergies, preferences, and religion. Eating halal food is a part of your identity and you should be proud of who you are.

Q: Ever since we studied the attack on the World Trade Center at school, kids have been picking on me. They say it's my fault all those people died because I'm a Muslim. This really hurts my feelings. How can I get help to stop the mean comments?

— *911 about 9/11*

A: I'm sorry that you are being bullied, 9. Your classmates need to know that there were Muslims who died when the World Trade Center was attacked. There were many brave first responders who were Muslim, and Muslim people who helped others to safety. When people say that all Muslims are responsible, they are stereotyping and hurtful. Ask a trusted teacher or school counsellor to speak to your class about the dangers of stereotypes and intolerance.

QUIZ

How do you handle Islamophobia?

When you are treated unfairly because of your beliefs, how do you respond? Are you **assertive** and clearly state what you need? Do you go on the offensive and get **aggressive?** Or are you **passive** in the face of Islamophobic behaviour and just let it happen? Take this quiz, then check out your answers to see how you act in the face of intolerance.

Passive

Aggressive

Assertive

1 Talking Trash

While walking with your friends to school you see them throwing garbage on the grounds of the mosque. Do you:

a) Join them and laugh? b) Say, "This isn't cool. I don't disrespect your faiths"? c) Shove them and threaten to come to their homes and dump all your garbage at their doors?

a) passive   b) assertive   c) aggressive

 ## 2 Refugee Ruckus

Your teacher starts talking about the recent arrival of Syrian refugees in your community and at your school. One of the kids in class says, "Terrorists shouldn't be allowed in Canada!" Do you:
a) Speak to your teacher and offer to tell the class about your experiences? b) Laugh and agree with your friends, even though you have family from Syria? c) Yell a profanity to your classmate and storm out of the classroom?

a) assertive   b) passive   c) aggressive

 ## 3 Cheesed Off

It's pizza day at school. Your cheese slice was given away by accident and all that is left is pepperoni pizza. Your friend says, "What's the big deal? Just take off the pepperoni." Do you:
a) Go hungry and grab a snack later? b) Ask the teacher to order another pizza, because you can't eat pizza that has had a pork product on it? c) Throw the pizza at the window?

a) passive   b) assertive   c) aggressive

 ## 4 Fickle Friends

You just started wearing a hijab to school this year. And now your friends are behaving all weird with you. They have stopped including you in their after-school plans and don't sit with you at lunch. Do you:
a) Go home and cry? b) Tell them how horrible they are and say you don't want to spend time with them anyway? c) Talk to your parents, guidance counsellor, or teacher about providing information about Islam and wearing the hijab?

a) passive   b) aggressive   c) assertive

 ## 5 Head Teacher

A classmate mentions a new law in Quebec that doesn't allow teachers to wear hijabs in school. She says the law is a good one and she wishes it applied to your school too. Do you:
a) Say nothing and don't mention that your mom wears a hijab? b) Explain how the law isn't inclusive and is bad for human rights? c) Tell your classmate to be quiet and no one wants to hear her opinions when she doesn't know what she's talking about?

a) passive   b) assertive   c) aggressive

 ## 6 Prayer Problem

It's time for prayers and praying will make you late for a math test. You feel like it's something you have to do even if it means being late. Do you:
a) Go to pray and decide to explain your lateness after? b) Skip the prayer and go to class? c) Go to pray and then blow off the test? How dare they schedule a test when they knew you had to pray!

a) assertive   b) passive   c) aggressive

---

7 To Grad or Not to Grad

It is your last year of middle school and you're excited about graduation. But you find out that the grad ceremonies will be held on the same day as Eid, a major holy day for Islam. You won't be able to go unless graduation is rescheduled. Do you:
a) Go home and cry? b) Send a mean tweet to the graduation committee calling them Islamophobic? c) Speak to your teacher and school principal about this inequity and what can be done about it?

a) passive   b) aggressive   c) assertive

---

8 New Kid

A new student arrives at your school. He is visibly Muslim and wears a long white shirt called a thobe. None of the kids want to play or sit with him at recess. They joke and call the new boy a terrorist when you are with them. Do you:
a) Sit with the new kid and get to know him? b) Do nothing and leave the new kid to fend for himself? c) Call your classmates names and tell them they're horrible people?

a) assertive   b) passive   c) aggressive

---

9 Forget the Festivities

Your school makes a big deal about Halloween festivities and has a huge parade. As a Muslim, you don't celebrate Halloween. Your teacher tells you that if you don't participate, you will be sent to the library with work while the rest of the class has a great time. Do you:
a) Feel furious and yell at your teacher? b) Speak to your teacher or principal about other options for kids not participating? c) Go to the library and work?

a) aggressive   b) assertive   c) passive

---

10 Tackling Dummy

Your Social Studies class is having a discussion about war, refugees, and immigration. Someone turns to you and asks, "So do Muslims believe in holy war?" Do you:
a) Yell at your classmate and call them a racist? b) Quietly say that you don't know? c) Tell them you can't speak for almost two billion people with their own opinions?

a) aggressive   b) passive   c) assertive

The **Believer**

You are not alone.

Even if you are the only Muslim kid in your class, everyone feels different in some way. Intolerance affects everyone, and anyone can look for a solution. As a Muslim, you might feel misunderstood and excluded. But remember that even though a problem might seem huge and unfixable, it can be fixed. You don't have to have the answers overnight but know that they will come. There are basic things you can do to make sure that you are not targeted for your belief or who you are.

Find better friends.
Even though it may seem impossible to choose between your friends and your faith, there are good people out there. You can choose your friends from them. If someone is being mean or discriminatory, they are not worth your friendship.

Know yourself and your faith.
When you are strong in your identity and who you are, no one can bring you down. Know why you chose to wear something, practise your faith the way you do, eat what you eat, and know that you don't have to answer to others for it. You have the right to practise your faith in peace.

Remember that people are still learning.
Not everyone who does or says something Islamophobic is being mean on purpose. Sometimes people might ask a question because they are curious and want to learn more. That doesn't mean they are being rude. Make sure you talk about things from a calm and cool manner. And when people make assumptions or ask you to provide answers on behalf of all Muslims, just know that you can speak only for yourself and not one-fifth of the whole world.

DID YOU KNOW?

- October is Islamic History Month in Canada.

- More than 90 per cent of Muslims in America are proud to be American.

Find a trusted adult.
Sometimes a situation could be confusing and make you feel powerless. There are human rights laws that protect people and asking a trusted adult could help you find a solution to your problem that you may not have already considered.

dos and don'ts

✓ Do you. Be yourself without fear of anyone.

✓ Do try to stay calm when you are being treated unfairly.

✓ Do tell someone who can help.

✓ Do name the action: tell someone targeting you that what they said or did was Islamophobic.

✓ Do tell someone discriminating against you how it made you feel and the hurt they caused.

✓ Do find allies (friends or family who support you in your beliefs).

✓ Do continue to be kind and lead by example.

✗ Don't think you are alone in this. You have allies.

✗ Don't take it personally; people are making Islamophobic comments based on their own prejudices and not on you.

✗ Don't get into an argument. Sometimes people are trying to provoke you.

✗ Don't use violence. It doesn't help and only harms.

✗ Don't hang out with people who treat you unkindly.

✗ Don't read Islamophobic comments on social media.

✗ Don't let Islamophobic actions get the best of you.

• An estimated 89,000 Muslim soldiers died fighting for the British Army during World War I.

Wearing head coverings, fasting, praying...

Does it bug you when you have to deal with other people's religion?

You don't understand why people can't keep what they believe separate from daily life.

And what if you think what they believe is different and strange?

DEAR DR. SHRINK-WRAPPED...

Q: My friend has dared me to write "Muslims Suck" in permanent marker on the school bathroom wall. I'm afraid that if I don't write it, my friend won't like me and will call me a sissy, but if I do it, I may get in trouble for writing on the wall.
—*Truth or Dare*

A: My worry is not about the wall, Truth, that can always be painted over. Imagine how the Muslim kids in your school would feel if they saw it. Imagine how you would feel if this was about you, or if they knew it was you who wrote it. It is more important to say "no" to something that takes away from your goodness, even if it is the harder thing to do.

dos and don'ts

✓ Do get to know more about Islam from credible sources.

✓ Do visit a mosque to ask questions about things that may confuse you.

✓ Do get to know someone before you judge them.

✓ Do remember that one person doesn't represent an entire group of people.

✓ Do know that even among Muslims there are many differences.

✓ Do learn more about the similarities between Islam and your beliefs.

✓ Do ask a Muslim person a question if you are genuinely trying to learn.

✓ Do better once you know better.

✗ Don't judge all Muslims based on prejudice.

✗ Don't exclude someone because you're uncomfortable with them.

✗ Don't hurt someone for being different from you.

✗ Don't let yourself get drawn into making Islamophobic comments online because you think it doesn't hurt anyone.

✗ Don't get carried away by hate.

✗ Don't go along with someone else who is being Islamophobic.

✗ Don't be too hard on yourself once you know better.

QUIZ

Do you have trouble with people who are different from you?

Whether it's because of what you think of groups of people, or because you are afraid and suspicious of them, are you saying and doing things that exclude and hurt people? Take this quiz to see what you can find out about yourself.
Of the following statements, how many are true and how many false?

1. I have the right to judge other people.

2. All people should believe what I believe.

3. I have been accused of being an Islamophobe.

4. I tend to blame others for the problems in the world.

5. I believe religion has no place in everyday life.

6. I don't trust people who don't think the way I do.

7. There should be laws so that people are all the same.

8. My friends are all the same as me.

9. My religious beliefs are the only ones that are right.

10. My religion tells me to do whatever I can to change people who believe the wrong things.

11. I have laughed at jokes about people from other countries.

12. I have told jokes about people of different religions.

13. I believe that things they say about other religions on TV must be true.

14. People should learn the national language when they move here.

15. People in head scarves make me uncomfortable.

16. Muslims don't like the way we live.

17. I could never date someone who wasn't the same as me.

18. I wish people would go back to where they came from.

19. Islam doesn't belong in this country.

20. People new to our country should learn to fit in.

21. I don't think someone's religion should have a say in what they eat.

22. People should pray on their own time.

23. I wish we had laws that made people not wear their religious clothing.

24. It's not racist to talk about Muslims.

25. Muslims are a violent people.

26. I don't know any Muslims.

27. Muslims don't like our freedom.

28. I could never be friends with a Muslim kid.

29. Change is hard for me.

30. Admitting mistakes is even harder for me.

Did you score a lot of Trues? Maybe you should talk to someone in your life (a parent, teacher, or faith leader) about how to become a more tolerant, respectful person.

Do you want to be part of the problem or part of the solution?

Try to imagine what it would feel like if people made assumptions about you and treated you badly based on what you believe. Your attitudes might be making things harder for people around you. But there are many things you can do to make things better for them and you.

Get to Know a Muslim

If you have negative views or thoughts about Muslims as a group of people, the best way to overcome this is to talk to a Muslim person. Feel free to ask respectfully about what they believe. You will be surprised to know they are actually a lot like you.

Visit a Mosque

Many mosques host community, open house, and information events. Feel free to reach out to the local leader of a mosque, called an imam, to give you a tour and answer any questions you may have.

When in Doubt, Ask!

If you aren't sure if something is offensive to someone, but you want to do right, you can ask. But be careful. How you ask a question about something personal is as important as the question you ask. You need to do it respectfully because you don't want to sound like you're being rude or intolerant. For example, you could politely ask a girl or woman wearing a head scarf what it means. You definitely shouldn't ask her what she is hiding under her hijab.

DID YOU KNOW?

- Muslim NHL players include Alain Nasreddine, Nail Yakupov, and Nazem Kadri.

Remember that Diversity is Strength

Can you imagine how boring life would be if we all looked the same, dressed the same, prayed the same, spoke the same, and ate the same? New people generate new ideas and new things. Throughout history, many great inventions and new innovations came from Muslim people who contributed to knowledge in math, science, astronomy, medicine, art, language, literacy, and philosophy.

When Social Media is Involved

It isn't hard to find comments about Muslims on social media or online spaces. But just because it is widely shared or retweeted doesn't mean the information is reliable, accurate or even true. Everyone follows and can post to social media. But since some people post a lot, and some people don't post at all, social media might not really reflect what most people think and feel. To truly understand if what you are reading can be trusted and is accurate, you have to ask yourself some questions.

- Who is the author? Is the person hiding their identity or giving a name and contact information in case you need more information?
- Where does it come from? Is the article or news story from a publisher like The New York Times or CBC News? Or is it some random person promoting a stereotype with nothing to back it up?
- What is the point of view? If the poster is trying to convince you of an opinion without sharing other views, then you should question it.
- Who stands to gain? Remember that online influencers are about business, not truth. If there are advertisers, the poster gets paid to put the ads in front of as many people as possible.

What can you do when you see Islamophobia online? We can all be allies. You have the power to change the negative stereotypes using social media.

- Remember that people don't know what they don't know. Counter lies with truth. Respond to negative posts with positive ones.
- If someone is creating posts that are hateful in your school or community, report it. Speak to a trusted adult and get them to help you address Islamophobic attitudes.
- Contact the owner or creator of the site and tell them what you are reading is very hateful and divisive. If people get in touch with them, it might motivate them to delete those posts.
- Share good news articles, books, and stories you hear about Muslims. When people hear just one side of the story, that's all they will believe. Put stories of Muslims who do good out there so people can see that they are more than the stereotype.
- Don't retweet or share fake news or articles. Reposting negative stereotypes, even if it is to say they are lies, only makes it worse.

- Muslim sports heroes include Hakeem Olajuwon (NBA), Shaquille O'Neal (NBA), Muhammad Ali (boxing), and Kareem Abdul-Jabbar (NBA).

- Ibtihaj Muhammad, a fencer from the US, was the first Olympian to compete while wearing a hijab.

The **Bystander**

Have you seen someone being bullied or harassed because they are Muslim?

Does it bother you when people talk about immigrants and refugees like they are a threat?

You realize that people should speak up when these sorts of incidents happen to them, but did you say or do anything?

Well, why not?

As a bystander, you have the power to choose action to stop Islamophobia.

If you turn away or quietly watch, you let the person who is being hateful and Islamophobic continue.

The easiest way to stop Islamophobia is to:

- Tell the person to stop what they are saying or doing that is unacceptable.

- Name the behaviour. Say, "What you're doing is hurtful and Islamophobic."

- Explain how their behaviour is hurtful. You could say, "When you do that, it makes them feel unsafe."

- Change the behaviour. You could say, "Next time, keep your hands to yourself."

- Help the person who is hurt. Ask if they are okay. You don't even need to talk to them, just go be near them.

- Report it. Tell a trusted adult about what you witnessed.

When you choose action, you make the world a safer place. Bullies go after one person because it is easy, so be the friend that someone else needs.

dos and don'ts

✓ Do ask the person being harmed if they want help.

✓ Do support the person harmed.

✓ Do assume best intentions of others.

✓ Do stand with or be near the person being harmed.

✓ Do call an adult who can help (teacher, parent, police officer).

✓ Do leave a situation that feels dangerous. Take the other person with you.

✓ Do try to put yourself in someone else's shoes.

✓ Do be a caring person.

✓ Do offer your friendship.

✗ Don't encourage the Islamophobe by laughing or being quiet.

✗ Don't leave the person who is being harmed alone.

✗ Don't try to fight a bully.

✗ Don't antagonize a bully and get them even angrier.

✗ Don't brush the action off as a joke or make it seem like nothing.

✗ Don't alienate or single out a Muslim kid.

QUIZ

Do you really get it?

Now you know Islamophobia is wrong, and the next time you witness it you know what you have to do. But do you really? What would you do in the following situations? This quiz has no right or wrong answers, because each situation is unique. Your answers may be different from the ones given below, but they could be right under the circumstances.

1 New Neighbour

You notice the new kid who moved in next door wears traditional Muslim clothes. He sees you and your friends playing basketball in your driveway. You should:

- Ask him if he wants to come join the game.
- Go over and introduce yourself.
- Wait until your friends leave and then say hi.
- Do nothing. If he wants to make friends, he will.

2 Pray or Play

Abdul goes out of class at lunchtime to pray every day. Some kids make fun of him behind his back. What should you do?

- Ask a teacher or principal to set up an information session about Islam.
- Contact a guidance counsellor.
- Talk to the other kids and tell them that they are being Islamophobic and they should stop.
- Tell a teacher in an anonymous note.
- Nothing. What Abdul doesn't know won't hurt him.

3 Bus Brother

You're on the bus and you see a girl in a hijab being teased. What do you do?

- Nothing. You don't want the bullying to get worse and do not feel safe getting involved.
- Tell the bus driver that someone is being bullied.
- Move to sit next to the girl.
- Ask the girl if she is okay.
- Tell the people teasing her to stop.

4 Terror Talk

At school you are talking in small groups about current events. One of your classmates says, "It's those Muslims. They're all terrorists." You should:

- Stay silent but shake your head at the ignorance of the statement.
- Let your teacher know about the comment.
- Tell them the comment is Islamophobic and has no place in a respectful talk.
- Find facts that show what the person said is not true.

5 Festive Food

You're on the planning committee for the school Carnival Day. You notice that most of the food vendors don't have halal meat or vegetarian options. You should:

- Ask your Muslim classmates about what they can eat.
- Go ahead with the options you have, but add some veggie burgers to the orders so anyone can have them.
- Encourage the committee to look for alternative food options.

Continues . . .

6 Party Line

Your friend is having a birthday party and has invited all the girls in the class except for Jannah, who is Muslim, because she thinks that Jannah won't belong. You should:

- Not say anything because it's not your party.
- Share your ideas for a guest list with your friend and include Jannah.
- Ask your friend if she could include Jannah too.
- Tell your friend you won't be coming to her party and ask Jannah if she wants to come over to your place instead, so she doesn't feel alone.

7 Ramadan Run

You are on the track team, and your school has planned a track and field meet during Ramadan. One of your best runners will be fasting that day. You decide to:

- Say nothing. The fasting athlete can speak for themselves.
- Encourage the athlete to let the track and field organizer know that he will be fasting.
- Ask the organizer if the dates of the track and field meet can be changed.
- Get someone from the Muslim community to come and talk to teachers and students about Ramadan.

DID YOU KNOW?

- There have been many Muslim female presidents in countries, such as Singapore, Indonesia, Kosovo, Turkey, Kyrgyzstan, Bangladesh, Pakistan, Senegal, Mali, Mauritius, and others.

8 Refugee Raging

You hear one of the older kids at recess telling a Muslim classmate that she is a refugee that "drains the system" and to go back to where she came from. What do you do?

- Nothing. It's not your business and you don't feel safe getting involved.
- Ask your classmate if she is okay.
- Tell a trusted adult.
- Ask your teacher if you can share a YouTube video about your country's role in welcoming refugees with the school.
- If you feel safe doing it, tell the older kid to stop making Islamophobic comments.

9 Graffiti Gone

Someone has vandalized the local mosque, spray-painting hateful messages all over it. You've heard the mosque is now holding a fundraiser to fix all the damage. What do you decide?

- To do nothing if you don't feel safe getting involved.
- To donate some money and stay home.
- To attend the fundraiser to support fixing the damage.
- To let your friends know about the event and encourage them to come too.

10 Party On

You plan a party to celebrate the end of the school year at your home. All of your friends are invited. One of your friends wants to bring her hijabi (a female Muslim who wears a hijab) friend along. How do you react?

- You tell your friend that the guest list is set. And don't allow other guests to bring friends.
- You want to say no, but realize that's just not cool, so you let her come.
- You think, the more the merrier!
- You think this is a good time for you to get to know a new person better.

- Malcolm X was an American Muslim imam who understood that Islam was a religion for all races and hoped for peace among all people.

- The Aga Khan Museum in Toronto is an Islamic history and art museum.

More Help

It takes time and critical thinking to learn the skills and ideas in this book. There are many ways to support inclusiveness and to deal with conflicts about Islamophobia, but only you know what feels right for you in different situations.

If you want more information, or for someone to talk to, the following resources might help.

Help Lines
Kids Help Phone 1-800-668-6868

Naseeha Youth Helpline: 1-866-NASEEHA

NISA Helpline: 1-888-315-NISA (6472) info@nisahelpline.com

Websites
A Bystander's Guide to Standing up Against Islamophobic Harassment http://www.themarysue.com/bystanders-harassment-guide

Muslim Youth Canada https://ccmw.com/youth/mycanada

MVSLIM https://mvslim.com

Naseeha North America https://naseeha.org

Books
Dear World: A Syrian Girl's Story of War and Plea for Peace by Bana Alabed, Simon & Schuster, 2017

Every Day Is Malala Day by Rosemary McCarney and Plan International, Second Story Press, 2014

The Hijab Boutique by Michelle Khan, The Islamic Foundation, 2011

The Breadwinner by Deborah Ellis, Groundwood Books, 2000

The Grand Mosque of Paris by Karen Gray Ruelle and Deborah Durland Desaix, Holiday House, 2010

A Long Pitch Home by Natalie Dias Lorenzi, Charlesbridge, 2016

Malcolm Little: The Boy Who Grew Up to Become Malcolm X by Ilyasah Shabazz, Atheneum Books for Young Readers, 2014

The Amazing Discoveries of Ibn Sina by Fatima Sharafeddine, Groundwood Books, 2015

My Name Was Hussein by Hristo Kyuchukov, Boyds Mills Press, 2004

The Roses in My Carpets by Rukhsana Khan, Fitzhenry & Whiteside, 2004

Muslim Child by Rukhsana Khan, Dundurn, 2001

Science, Medicine and Math in the Early Islamic World by Trudee Romanek, Crabtree Publishing, 2012

Videos
14 and Muslim https://www.14andmuslim.com

This video looks at how ideas of diversity and tolerance play out in the Canadian classroom

Salaam B'y https://www.salaamby.ca/educators

This film, screened in over fifty cities internationally, follows the coming of age story of Muslim Newfoundlander Aatif Baskanderi

Wrap My Hijab, Rap Video by Mona Hayder https://youtu.be/XOX9O_kVPeo

TED Talks: What does my headscarf mean to you? https://www.ted.com/talks/yassmin_abdel_magied_what_does_my_headscarf_mean_to_you?utm_campaign=tedspread&utm_medium=referral&utm_source=tedcomshare

Copyright © 2020 by Safia Saleh
Illustrations © 2020 by James Lorimer & Company

Published in Canada in 2020.
Published in the United States in 2021.

James Lorimer & Company Ltd., Publishers acknowledges funding support from the Ontario Arts Council (OAC), an agency of the Government of Ontario. We acknowledge the support of the Canada Council for the Arts, which last year invested $153 million to bring the arts to Canadians throughout the country. This project has been made possible in part by the Government of Canada and with the support of Ontario Creates.

Series design: Blair Kerrigan/Glyphics
Cover design: Gwen North
Cover image: Shutterstock

Library and Archives Canada Cataloguing in Publication

Title: Islamophobia : deal with it in the name of peace / Safia Saleh ; illustrated by Hana Shafi.
Names: Saleh, Safia, author. | Shafi, Hana, 1993- illustrator.
Series: Deal with it (Toronto, Ont.)
Description: Series statement: Deal with it
Identifiers: Canadiana (print) 20200199161 | ISBN 9781459415386 (hardcover)
Subjects: LCSH: Islamophobia—Juvenile literature. | LCSH: Religious discrimination—Juvenile literature. | LCSH: Religious tolerance—Juvenile literature.
Classification: LCC BP52 .S25 2020 | DDC j305.6/97—dc23

James Lorimer & Company Ltd., Publishers
117 Peter Street, Suite 304
Toronto, ON, Canada, M5V 0M3
www.lorimer.ca

Distributed in Canada by:
Formac Lorimer Books
5502 Atlantic Street
Halifax, NS, Canada
B3H 1G4
www.formaclorimerbooks.ca

Distributed in the US by:
Lerner Publisher Services
1251 Washington Ave. N.
Minneapolis, MN, USA
55401
www.lernerbooks.com

Printed and bound in China.